OECD and CCET *Economic Surveys* 1997
Electronic Books

The OECD *Economic Surveys*, both for the Member countries and for countries of Central and Eastern Europe covered by the Organisation's Centre for Co-operation with Economies in Transition, are also published as electronic books – incorporating the text, tables and figures of the printed version. The information will appear on screen in an identical format, including the use of colour in graphs.

The electronic book, which retains the quality and readability of the printed version throughout, will enable readers to take advantage of the new tools that the ACROBAT software (included with the diskette) provides by offering the following benefits:

❑ User-friendly and intuitive interface
❑ Comprehensive index for rapid text retrieval, including a table of contents, as well as a list of numbered tables and figures
❑ Rapid browse and search facilities
❑ Zoom facility for magnifying graphics or for increasing page size for easy readability
❑ Cut and paste capabilities
❑ Printing facility
❑ Reduced volume for easy filing/portability

Working environment: DOS, Windows or Macintosh

Subscription 97: FF 1 800   US$317   £230   DM 550

Complete 1995 series on CD-ROM:
FF 2 000   US$365   £255   DM 600

Complete 1996 series on CD-ROM (to be issued early 1997):
FF 2 000   US$365   £255   DM 600

Please send your order to OECD Publications 2, rue André-Pascal 75775 PARIS CEDEX 16 France or, preferably, to the Centre or bookshop with whom you placed your initial order for this Economic Survey.

OECD
ECONOMIC
SURVEYS

1997-1998

MEXICO

ORGANISATION FOR ECONOMIC CO-OPERATION AND DEVELOPMENT

ORGANISATION FOR ECONOMIC CO-OPERATION AND DEVELOPMENT

Pursuant to Article 1 of the Convention signed in Paris on 14th December 1960, and which came into force on 30th September 1961, the Organisation for Economic Co-operation and Development (OECD) shall promote policies designed:

- to achieve the highest sustainable economic growth and employment and a rising standard of living in Member countries, while maintaining financial stability, and thus to contribute to the development of the world economy;
- to contribute to sound economic expansion in Member as well as non-member countries in the process of economic development; and
- to contribute to the expansion of world trade on a multilateral, non-discriminatory basis in accordance with international obligations.

The original Member countries of the OECD are Austria, Belgium, Canada, Denmark, France, Germany, Greece, Iceland, Ireland, Italy, Luxembourg, the Netherlands, Norway, Portugal, Spain, Sweden, Switzerland, Turkey, the United Kingdom and the United States. The following countries became Members subsequently through accession at the dates indicated hereafter: Japan (28th April 1964), Finland (28th January 1969), Australia (7th June 1971), New Zealand (29th May 1973), Mexico (18th May 1994), the Czech Republic (21st December 1995), Hungary (7th May 1996), Poland (22nd November 1996) and the Republic of Korea (12th December 1996). The Commission of the European Communities takes part in the work of the OECD (Article 13 of the OECD Convention).

Publié également en français.

Table of contents

Boxes

Tables

Figures

BASIC STATISTICS OF MEXICO

THE LAND

Area (sq. km)	1 967 183	Inhabitants in major cities (thousands, 1990):	
Agricultural area (sq. km) (1990)	394 600	Mexico City	15 048
		Guadalajara	3 044
		Monterrey	2 651

THE PEOPLE

Population (thousands, 1996)	96 582	Employment (thousands, 1995)	33 881
Inhabitants per sq. km (1996)	49.1		
Annual population growth (1980-1996)	2.1		

PRODUCTION

Structure of production		GDP (US$ billion, 1996)	329.4
(per cent of total, 1996):		GDP per capita (US$, using PPPs, 1996)	7 776.5
Agriculture	5.4	Gross fixed capital formation	
Industry	30.2	(per cent of GDP, 1996)	17.2
of which: Manufacturing	19.7		
Services	64.4		

THE GOVERNMENT

			Chamber
General government consumption		Composition of Parliament	
(per cent of GDP, 1996)	10.1	(1997):	Senate / of Deputies
Federal government capital expenditure		PRI	77 / 238
(per cent of GDP, 1996)	1.9	PAN	33 / 121
Federal government revenue		PRD	16 / 126
(per cent of GDP, 1996)	15.4	Other	2 / 15
Public sector debt (per cent of GDP, 1996)	25.1		

FOREIGN TRADE

Exports of goods and services		Imports of goods and services	
(per cent of GDP, 1996)	31.5	(per cent of GDP, 1996)	29.0
Main exports (per cent of total, 1996):		Main imports (per cent of total, 1996):	
Manufactures	83.7	Intermediate goods	80.4
Petroleum products	12.1	Capital goods	12.2
Agriculture	3.7	Consumer goods	7.4

THE CURRENCY

Monetary unit: Peso	Currency units per US dollar, average of daily figures:	
	Year 1996	7.60
	November 1997	8.28

Note: An international comparison of certain basic statistics is given in an Annex table.

This Survey is based on the Secretariat's study prepared for the annual review of Mexico by the Economic and Development Review Committee on 26th November 1997.

•

After revisions in the light of discussions during the review, final approval of the Survey for publication was given by the Committee on 15th December 1997.

•

The previous Survey of Mexico was issued in December 1996.

Assessment and recommendations

The recovery from the 1995 recession is accelerating and spreading across sectors...

When Mexico was last reviewed towards the end of 1996, the economy was embarked on an export-led recovery from the sharp recession of 1995. In the first half of 1997, output growth quickened and its base broadened, as the recovery spread to domestic-oriented sectors. Exports and investment continued to grow rapidly, while private consumption, which had been lagging, picked up. Nonetheless, in the middle of 1997 household consumption was still below its pre-crisis level in real terms. Job creation in the formal sector of the economy has been substantial over the past twelve months, and real average earnings stopped falling around mid-1997; they were then about 20 per cent below their 1994 level. CPI inflation has declined to 18 per cent in October 1997, year on year, down from around 28 per cent in December 1996. Mirroring the recovery of domestic demand, merchandise imports gained momentum, and the current account deficit widened in the second half of 1996 and during 1997, against a background of increasing net capital inflows from abroad, a stable nominal exchange rate and rising currency reserves.

... and prospects for sustained growth in the short-term are favourable

In a context of strengthening business and household confidence, the present policy setting – prudent fiscal policy and a firm commitment to continued disinflation – is conducive to sustained growth in the future, notwithstanding some slowdown in the very near term as the process of recuper-

1

ating from the 1995 slump comes to an end. Recent developments suggest that growth should continue at rates of 5 to 6 per cent and be more evenly spread across the economy; and inflation is expected to continue to decline to 12 per cent by the end of 1998 (year on year). This environment should support sustained job creation in the formal economy, inducing a shift of labour from informal activities to better remunerated occupations in the formal sector. Wage pressures may emerge in the manufacturing export sector, but overall labour market slack, as evidenced by a still large stock of workers in low productivity activities in the informal sector and in rural areas, is likely to exert a moderating influence on average earnings. Although cost-competitiveness may gradually worsen under the Secretariat's usual technical assumption of unchanged nominal exchange rates, Mexico's export performance over the last year or so suggests that there are favourable non-price factors at play, the influence of which is likely to persist. Sustained import growth, nevertheless, is expected to translate into a widening of the current account deficit – from some US6\frac{1}{2}$ billion this year to a little over US$12 billion in 1998 (around 2$\frac{1}{2}$ per cent of GDP).

However, some risks and uncertainties are attached to the outlook

Several developments are a source of concern at this juncture. Although the balance sheets of both banks and debtors have improved, the level of non-performing loans remains uncomfortably high, hindering bank lending and private expenditure (see below). Continuation of a swift income recovery and a further decline in real and nominal interest rates are key ingredients of a sound solution to the problem. Another risk is related to uncertainties about the import intensity of a rapid and broad recovery of domestic demand. Given the pivotal role played by current account imbalances in past exchange rate crises, the authorities are concerned with keeping the current account deficit within a sustainable range, the level of which is dependent on the composition of capital inflows. Upward pressure on the exchange rate created by accelerating capital inflows would exacerbate this concern, especially if these inflows were of a short-term (*i.e.* speculative) nature. The extent to which higher labour demand induced by projected output growth will continue to translate into employment expansion rather than into real wage rises remains uncertain. On the other hand, strong labour productivity growth and persistent overall labour market slack reduce the risk of cost-push inflation.

The requirements for monetary policy seem clear...

Given the still high consumer price increases it is essential for monetary policy to continue to focus on reducing inflation, building on recent achievements, while at the same time aiming at maintaining stable conditions in financial markets. A steady move to lower inflation would bring nominal and real interest rates down further, which would help to alleviate the balance-sheet problems still affecting private sector agents and strengthen investment. The monetary policy framework, discussed in some detail in the Survey, is centred around an unambiguous commitment by the Central Bank to bring down inflation: the monetary programme announced at the start of each year sets the inflation target for the year, while the stock of primary money is used as an intermediate target, subject to an international reserve constraint. The more detailed policy formulation, increased transparency and better communication about the rationale for policy actions should be helpful in promoting market confidence, while instruments to facilitate monetary management have been refined. A fundamental difference from the situation prevailing before December 1994 is the floating currency regime now in vigour. Flexibility of the currency reduces the predictability of effective returns on short-term (speculative) foreign

3

investments, thereby reducing their attractiveness. Moreover, as trade imbalances increase, they are likely to induce countervailing exchange rate changes before current account deficits become overwhelming. Building up a track record of inflation control can further strengthen credibility of monetary policy, which is crucial to ensure financial market stability, thereby helping to avoid sudden reversals in international capital flows and their disruptive repercussion on the domestic economy.

... and a cautious fiscal policy stance should be maintained

The public sector financial balance is close to zero and expected to remain so, while the net public debt (at around 30 per cent of GDP at the end of 1996) is low by international comparison and continues to fall relative to GDP. With the recovery of demand well established, the cyclical position would require a cautious fiscal policy stance. Prudent management of public finances also has the advantage of preserving room for manoeuvre in the event of adverse developments as well as fostering market confidence in government policy. The solid output growth projected, if it materialises, will tend to increase tax receipts, thereby allowing an increase in spending – which is still needed to correct for the drastic 1995 cuts – without jeopardising budget balance. A margin of safety is provided by the prudent assumptions (regarding output growth, world oil prices and the international environment) on which the budget projections are based. In the longer-run, however, fiscal policy faces a number of challenges, discussed in the government's medium-term programme.

The government's medium-term scenario provides guidance for macro-policy...

In its National Programme for Financing Development, 1995-2000, presented in June 1997, the government outlines the principles that will guide policy making over the remaining period of its administration, sketching a quantitative scenario for main macroeconomic variables. Setting a medium-term benchmark for the conduct of policy can help anchor market expectations and strengthen investors' confidence in the policy strategy of the government. The government scenario is cautious in its projection of output growth and the path of disinflation outlined (explicitly defined as an upper bound rather than a target). Drawing the lesson from past crises, the programme focuses on the external current account constraint and the insufficiency of domestic saving. Whereas foreign saving can complement domestic saving, the extent to which investment can reliably be financed through capital inflows ultimately depends on the stability of these flows: foreign direct investment typically carries less risk of sudden reversals than more volatile portfolio investments or banking flows. There is little that policy can do to influence the type of capital inflow directly, although by securing a stable environment for investment, it can induce higher levels of long-term capital inflows.

... stressing the importance of high domestic saving...

The programme stresses the role structural reforms can play to loosen the external constraint on growth by creating favourable conditions for higher private saving in the longer run. The pension reform, which introduced privately managed individual retirement saving accounts represents a transition from a pay-as-you-go to a funded system. By offering the possibility to make voluntary contributions to these accounts, it might further stimulate the expansion of private saving. The growth of a retail deposit market, likely to result from increased competition in the banking sector, as well as the development of small savings institutions, can help to capture saving from the population at large and channel them to their most productive use.

... including a substantial contribution from public saving

Significant public saving will have to be maintained to enhance domestic saving. The government's contingent liabilities with respect to the banking sector support and the cost of the social security reform, as well as the budget's sensitivity to unanticipated exogenous shocks (such as changes in oil prices and foreign interest rates), also point to the need to maintain strong public finances over the medium term. At the same time, there are large public spending needs in physical and human capital investment in Mexico. The way to meet both requirements – a broadly-balanced budget and rapid expansion of infrastructure investment and key programmes in basic education, health care and poverty alleviation – is to act on two fronts simultaneously: efforts to reallocate budget resources towards priority areas should be continued as planned while seeking to enhance the effectiveness of public spending. At the same time, tax receipts – which, as a proportion of GDP, are the lowest in the OECD area –will need to increase. Efforts underway to raise the effectiveness of the tax collection system – by modernising tax administration and reducing tax avoidance – can contribute. If results of current reforms fall short of expectations, adjustments to the tax system should not be ruled out. It is clearly preferable to increase tax revenue by broadening the tax base rather than by raising tax rates; and for an open economy like Mexico, minimising tax disincentives *vis-à-vis* its main trading partner, the United States, is particularly important. In this context, it should be noted that a substantial share of government revenue comes (through the PEMEX contribution) from oil exploitation, which in economic terms represents a run-down of non-renewable resources. This concern underlies the administration's explicit plan to give more weight to (non-oil) taxes in budget revenue; such a shift would also reduce the budget's vulnerability to changes in world oil prices.

The government remains committed to structural reform...

The government has advanced further on structural initiatives put in place in recent years. Efforts to enhance basic education achievements and to provide support to the poorest segments of the population have been intensified. The focus on educating the rural poor, embodied in programmes that link support for basic education, health and nutrition, is appropriate; such programmes can contribute to reduce the very large differentials in development that exist across regions by raising labour efficiency in rural areas. Although the labour market has demonstrated its flexibility in coping with severe shocks, practices and regulations regarding hiring and firing will need to continue to evolve because initiatives aimed at enhancing the flexibility of employment in the formal sector can contribute to lowering barriers that keep many activities in the informal sector. The improved economic situation and important changes in the political scene may open a window of opportunity that the social partners should seize with a view to modernising institutional arrangements. Further progress has been made in opening key sectors of the economy (railroads, satellite communications, natural gas and electricity) to private initiative. Increased participation of private entrepreneurs (domestic and foreign) in these sectors, through concessions or outright sale of state enterprises, should allow an expansion of the country's infrastructure under the public sector budget constraint. However, competition needs to take place on a level playing field for these measures to bring about their full efficiency gains and the associated benefits to other sectors of the economy.

... while seeking to strengthen institutional checks and balances

For economic reforms to bear fruit, it is essential that rules governing business activities be transparent, their application thorough, and pertinent public institutions independent and efficient. The administration, in the National Development Plan 1995-2000, acknowledged that reforms were

7

needed in the public administration to foster transparency and accountability. The growing openness of the Mexican political scene bodes well for achieving a stronger system of institutional checks and balances. Initial steps, especially the greater independence granted to the civil service, have already been taken, and efforts are underway to reform internal security and the judiciary system.

The fiscal cost of bank rescue has increased

The various support programmes for banks introduced in the aftermath of the peso crisis have succeeded in strengthening the banks' balance sheets, increasing capitalisation ratios and reserves. Through the purchase of loan portfolios to support banks and the take-over of poorly capitalised or badly managed banks, about a third of total bank assets and of the stock of bank loans has come under control of the agency in charge of dealing with insolvent banks (FOBAPROA). The authorities believe that there will be no need for additional action, but the ultimate cost of the whole package of support operations already implemented – currently estimated at 11.9 per cent of 1997 GDP, of which 2.2 percentage points have been covered – is difficult to quantify with any certainty. While non-performing loans are now expanding at a lower rate, it is difficult to gauge how quickly remaining balance-sheet problems will be resolved. The sustained recovery of the economy that is projected, together with a continued decline in interest rates, should help firms and households to further correct their over-indebtedness, thereby facilitating the return to normal relationships between debtors and creditors and creating conditions for a revival of bank credit in the course of 1998.

An overhaul of the health care system is under way...

Despite improvements in the overall health status of the Mexican population over past decades, there are substantial opportunities for further progress, especially in terms of reducing the considerable disparities in health outcomes among regions and socio-economic groups within Mexico. Recognised problems of inequity, inefficiency and poor quality of medical services have led the authorities to engage in a major reform of the system. The strategy aims at moving away from the current segmented system, made up of parallel sub-systems, each catering to a specific population group. While total spending on health care is not high by international comparison, the system typically left a large segment of the population (10 million people) with no access to health care. There is dissatisfaction with the quality of medical services provided by the national health system; and people from all income categories have recourse to private services of unequal quality, generally implying out-of-pocket payments. Moreover, in the longer run upward spending pressures are likely to intensify. The reform strategy comprises three main objectives: expanding coverage, containing costs and raising quality of services.

... proceeding gradually on several fronts

An important first step has already been taken to extend the coverage of basic health care with the delivery of a package of essential health care services to the extremely poor in remote areas (benefiting 6 million people in 1997). With the on-going decentralisation of health care to states, norms are being set for the state provision of services to the uninsured. Changes in the financing of the main public health insurance (IMSS) have lowered required contributions to the compulsory health insurance scheme for people engaged in formal activities, as well as the cost of voluntary participation in the system; both measure are expected to attract more households into the social security system – people hitherto uninsured but who have a capacity to pay.

While long-term goals seem indisputable, important decisions are still to be taken

In the longer run, the reform aims at ensuring universal access to basic medical care; but what should constitute the minimum set of health services available to all remains to be defined. Ultimately, the reformed system is to be organised by functions, with the Ministry of Health conducting national health policy and being responsible for the regulation of, and norm-setting for, the whole system, while many providers – public as well as private – would compete to deliver services. The list of required changes to move in that direction is long. Increasing the autonomy of hospitals and the transparency of their budgets is necessary before splitting the functions of purchaser and provider of health services. Introducing competition at the general practitioner level by giving patients in urban areas free choice of family doctor is also of strategic importance. One of the key planks in the IMSS reform aims at introducing some competition by allowing social security beneficiaries to opt out of the system and to receive health services from managed care organisations that would receive financial resources from social security funds. The reimbursement will be independent of individual or firm-level contributions to preserve the solidarity element, but regulations need to be adopted to prevent undue fiscal risk and the creation of a two-tier system.

Summary

The recovery of the Mexican economy has gained momentum, in a context of a monetary policy committed to further disinflation and prudent fiscal policy. While prospects for continued growth and disinflation appear favourable in the short term, the external constraint remains a concern for the medium-term outlook. However, to the extent that the current account deficit remains moderate and is financed by foreign direct investment and other long-term capital inflows, it should not constitute an impediment to sustainable growth. The rapid output growth that Mexico needs to absorb labour market slack – close to 6 per cent per year, according to the authorities – requires a high level of fixed investment. Stronger domestic saving is needed to finance it, so as to avoid relying too heavily on foreign borrowing, which, unless financed by long-term capital, would make the economy vulnerable to sudden shifts in confidence of foreign investors. While sustained income growth with low inflation is a necessary condition for higher private saving, some of the structural changes underway can also contribute. At the same time, the government needs to further enhance the effectiveness of taxation and public spending. Progress in these areas would help meet spending needs to catch up on long-standing gaps in physical and social infrastructure, while maintaining a strong fiscal position to face contingent liabilities. Current initiatives to reform the national health system hold the promise of a more equitable and efficient provision of health care services.

I. Recent trends and short-term prospects

Stimulated by buoyant exports and investment, real GDP has been growing at a sustained pace for two years since its rebound from the 1995 trough.[1] Over the same period, inflation and interest rates have been on a declining trend, and the current external account has recorded a small, though increasing, deficit (Figure 1). This favourable performance needs to be seen in perspective, however. Per capita real GDP did not return to its 1994 level until the second quarter of 1997; real wages fell by a cumulative 25 per cent in 1995-96, and private consumption, despite its acceleration in the first half of 1997, was still below its pre-recession level at mid-year.

The current economic cycle in perspective

The rebound of economic activity following the 1995 slump was more rapid than the recovery in the aftermath of the 1982 debt crisis (Figure 2). This greater responsiveness of the Mexican economy reflects the increased openness of the economy as well as enhanced flexibility engendered by the structural reforms implemented in recent years. Economic growth at first relied heavily on the exporting sector, predominantly involving larger firms, and was concentrated in certain geographic areas (North and Centre). But this pattern seems to have changed during the first half of 1997 as the recovery spread across sectors and regions.

Faced with the severe slump in domestic demand, many Mexican producers were able to re-orient their activities to foreign markets. Exports of goods and services grew in volume by a cumulative 60 per cent in 1995 and 1996, providing a stimulus to investment in exporting firms. The impulse that export activities can give to the domestic economy is, however, dampened by a heavy reliance on foreign inputs. In stark contrast to developments in 1982-83, when imports fell

Figure 1. **KEY ASPECTS OF ECONOMIC ACTIVITY**

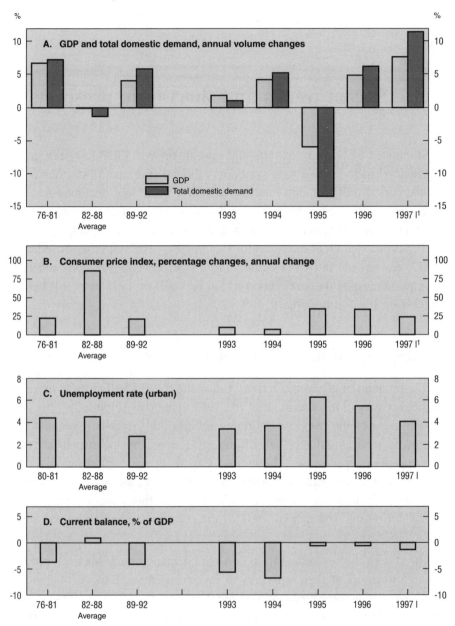

1. Changes from previous half-year (s.a.a.r).
Source: OECD and INEGI.

Table 1. Demand and output

Percentage changes, volume, 1993 prices

	1994 Current prices[1]	1989-93[2]	1994	1995	1996	1996 S2/ 1996 S1[3]	1997 S1/ 1996 S2[3]
Demand							
Private consumption	1 016.5	4.9	4.6	−9.5	2.3	1.2	7.8
Government consumption	164.2	3.0	2.9	−1.3	3.7	13.6	−1.5
Gross fixed capital formation	274.9	7.6	8.4	−29.0	17.7	20.7	21.8
Public sector	53.3	3.2	2.9	−19.7	24.7	−5.4	25.9
Private sector	221.5	9.0	9.8	−31.2	15.8	29.8	20.7
Final domestic demand	1 455.5	5.1	5.1	−12.3	4.8	5.8	9.1
Change in stockbuilding[4]	33.8	0.1	0.5	−2.1	1.7	0.9	2.9
Total domestic demand	1 489.3	5.1	5.5	−13.9	6.5	6.6	11.9
Exports of goods and services	236.4	5.8	17.4	33.0	18.7	26.3	8.3
Imports of goods and services	305.6	14.9	20.5	−12.8	27.8	31.9	23.4
Change in foreign balance[4]	−69.2	−1.3	−1.2	8.5	−1.2	−0.5	−3.5
GDP at market prices	1 420.2	3.8	4.4	−6.2	5.1	5.9	8.0

						1996 S2/ 1995 S2	1997 S1/ 1996 S1
Output							
Agriculture, forestry, fishing	78.2	2.0	0.9	1.0	1.2	−0.9	5.8
Mining (including petroleum)	17.4	1.4	2.5	−2.7	8.3	9.4	3.5
Manufacturing	245.0	4.3	4.1	−4.8	10.9	13.2	9.2
Construction	69.1	5.1	8.4	−23.5	11.4	20.8	10.1
Electricity	19.2	2.6	4.8	2.1	4.5	5.4	5.2
Commerce	275.7	4.5	6.8	−15.6	4.1	8.3	8.8
Transport and communication	124.8	4.2	8.7	−4.9	8.7	10.4	9.3
Financial services	211.5	4.5	5.4	−0.3	1.4	3.3	5.2
Community services	311.0	3.1	1.3	−2.3	1.0	2.5	3.8

1. Billion pesos.
2. Annual average growth rate.
3. Changes from previous half-year at annual rates (based on quarterly data seasonally adjusted by the OECD Secretariat).
4. As a percentage of GDP in the previous period.
Source: INEGI; OECD.

sharply and remained sluggish for several years, their decline in 1995 was modest and their recovery rapid, reflecting changes in the trade structure: exports of manufactured goods (including in-bond activities, which have a particularly high import content) accounted for over 80 per cent of total exports in 1996, while the share of oil had fallen to 12 per cent.[2]

Figure 2. **COMPARISON OF TWO CYCLES**

Volume indices of seasonally-adjusted data

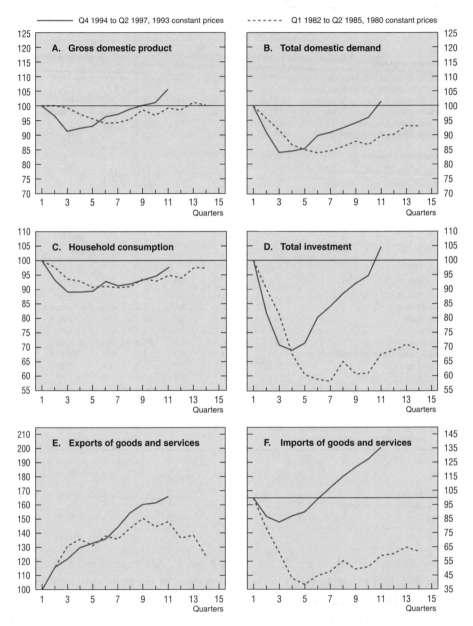

Source: OECD.

The recovery is becoming more broadly-based

In 1996, as domestic demand gradually recovered and imports picked up, the contribution of net exports to GDP growth turned negative, notwithstanding a continued rapid export expansion (Figure 3). The pattern of growth appears to have changed in the first half of 1997: while exports and investment continued to expand rapidly, private consumption, which had been lagging, picked up. With annual growth averaging 10 per cent in 1996 and 1997I, total aggregate demand (total domestic demand plus exports of goods and services) in 1997I was 9.5 per cent above its pre-crisis level; but its composition has changed significantly, with the domestic component down 8.7 percentage points to 77 per cent of aggregate demand in 1997I.

Gross fixed investment has been the most buoyant domestic demand component in the current cycle, expanding at annual rates close to 20 per cent during 1996 and in the first half of 1997. By mid-1997, it was still slightly below its 1994 level in real terms. The recovery of investment was driven by public sector projects and capital outlays of export-oriented firms. Against a background of unfavourable credit market conditions, investment in the export sector was financed by income from sales abroad and a significant contribution from increased foreign direct investment. Strong investment demand was reflected in rapid growth of domestic production of machinery and equipment (nearly 75 per cent of purchases of capital goods) as well as in rising imports of this category of goods (currently 14 per cent of imports, and expanding rapidly; Table 2). With reduced uncertainties and improved cash-flow, due to the recovery of activity and lower interest rates, firms oriented towards the domestic market appear also to have started increasing purchases of machinery and equipment beginning around mid-1997.

The launching of public works in 1996 – expansion of the electricity capacity, oil production projects and the development of federal highways – contributed to the recovery of the construction sector. On the other hand, balance-sheet-problems of firms and households inherited from the 1994/95 peso crisis and low expectations concerning domestic activity explain the dismal performance of private construction (residential and other) during 1996.[3] By mid-1997, however, first signs of an upturn in private construction had become manifest. New infrastructure projects in the 1997 budget are also contributing to

Figure 3. **CONTRIBUTIONS TO REAL GDP GROWTH**[1]

Percentage points

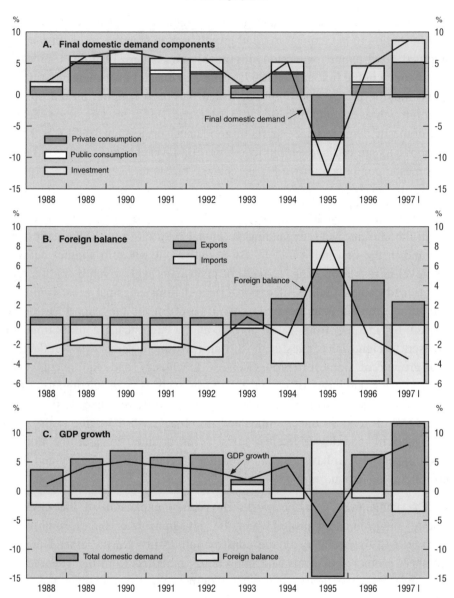

1. Changes as a percentage of real GDP in the previous period.
Source: OECD.

Table 2. **Indicators of investment activity**

Percentage changes from same period of previous year[1]

	1995	1996	1996				1997	
	Average	Average	Q1	Q2	Q3	Q4	Q1	Q2
Gross fixed capital formation	−29.0	17.7	−2.1	18.3	27.5	28.8	18.1	24.7
Machinery and equipment	−36.4	26.5	0.2	32.5	32.2	43.3	29.9	41.1
Residential building and construction	−22.5	11.4	−3.9	8.9	24.1	17.8	8.7	11.5
Domestic production of machinery and equipment	−12.4	18.7	3.2	28.5	21.5	23.5	20.1	18.9
Imports of capital goods	−34.7	25.6	−1.3	26.2	30.2	49.7	31.0	46.8

1. Volume, 1993 constant price basis for demand and ouptut; dollar values for trade data.
Source: INEGI.

the sector's expansion: investment projects directly financed from budget resources are being complemented by privately financed infrastructure projects, to be transferred to the public sector upon completion.

With the interruption of net capital inflows at the time of the 1994/95 peso crisis, investment had to be financed by gross domestic saving during 1995 and part of 1996. The situation started to change as foreign capital inflows resumed in the course of 1996. In the first half of 1997, gross capital formation including stockbuilding had reached 25.4 per cent of GDP at current prices, while domestic saving had risen to 24.6 per cent (a record level over the past 10 years), and foreign saving contributed less than 1 percentage point of GDP to investment financing (Table 3).

Private consumption remained weak until the first half of 1997, reflecting falling real wages. Retail sales, which had dropped by 20 per cent (in real terms) in 1995, remained flat during most of 1996, picking up only in the course of 1997.[4] Real wages suffered drastic cuts in 1995 and again in 1996, stabilising in the first half of 1997 and only increasing after mid-year. Employment, however, started to expand from the onset of the recovery, so that total remuneration of employees began to grow slightly as from 1996. Income from entrepreneurship is also likely to have benefited from the recovery, supporting household real disposable income. Households have reduced their indebtedness (the sector as a whole having returned to a net creditor position *vis-à-vis* the financial sector). Nonetheless, for many households, normal relations with banks have not yet been restored, impeding a recovery of spending through consumer credit.

19

Table 3. **Aggregate saving and investment**
Percentage of GDP

	1993	1994	1995	1996	1996 S1	1997 S1 [1]
Gross capital formation	21.0	21.7	19.6	20.9	22.0	25.4
Gross domestic saving	15.1	14.7	19.0	20.4	22.3	24.6
Public [2]	3.6	3.2	3.3	3.6	..	..
Private [3]	11.6	11.4	15.8	16.7	..	..
Foreign saving	5.9	7.0	0.6	0.6	−0.3	0.9

1. Preliminary.
2. The public sector comprises federal government and enterprises under budgetary control. The estimate is based on Ministry of Finance accounts.
3. The figure is obtained by substracting public saving from gross domestic saving.
Source: Banco de México; Ministry of Finance; OECD.

In real terms, aggregate household consumption in the first half of 1997 just reached its 1993 average level. In addition, the partial recovery has been concentrated on a limited segment of the population. Purchases of non-durables, which include necessity items (food, beverages) as well as clothing and footwear, continued to decline in 1996 and, in the second half of that year, were 9 per cent below their level in the same period of 1993, suggesting that the improvement in economic conditions had not yet reached the major part of the population.[5] By contrast, purchases of household durables (which represent only 10 per cent of private consumption, concentrated in the higher income categories) rebounded early in 1996, and by the second half of the year were above the corresponding 1993 levels. Despite a pick up in the first half of 1997 (including purchases of non-durables), per capita consumption remained well below pre-crisis levels. All in all, taking into account population growth over the past two years and the uneven distribution of income gains during the recovery, it is clear that in terms of general welfare, the setback of the 1995 recession is still far from having been compensated.

Labour market trends improve

After a dismal performance in 1995, the labour market situation improved significantly during the 1996 recovery. The number of insured employees – an indicator of activity in the formal sector – started to increase as from the beginning of 1996, steadily gaining momentum thereafter. By the third quarter of

1997, the number of permanent workers insured by the IMSS had expanded by 1.8 million (or 21 per cent) from its mid-1995 trough, exceeding the 1994 level. The manufacturing sector accounted for about half of this increase. Within the sector, employment in *maquiladoras* (in-bond industries), which had continued to expand at a quick pace even in 1995, accelerated during 1996 and the first half of 1997, so that by mid-year, the sector accounted for 30 per cent of total manufacturing employment. Other manufacturing enterprises, construction and the service sector started to record significant employment growth only in the second half of 1996 (Table 4).

Table 4. **Labour market indicators**

	1993	1994	1995	1996	1996 S1	1996 S2	1997 S1
	Thousands	Percentage changes from same period of previous year					
Insured employment							
(private sector)	**11 318**	**1.1**	**−4.2**	**3.7**	**0.3**	**7.1**	**8.9**
Permanent	10 033	1.4	−1.6	4.8	2.3	7.2	8.7
Manufacturing	2 967	−0.8	−2.4	7.0	3.0	11.0	12.1
Construction	282	2.8	−18.3	0.8	−7.2	10.2	13.4
Trade	1 704	1.4	−3.1	1.4	−1.8	4.6	6.8
Personal services	1 671	1.9	−1.9	2.7	−0.3	5.7	10.5
Temporary	1 286	−1.4	−24.4	−7.7	−18.4	5.5	11.0
Employment in manufacturing							
Non-maquiladoras		−3.1	−9.1	2.2	−0.4	5.1	5.1
Maquiladoras		7.6	11.2	16.4	13.9	18.9	19.9
	Per cent						
Urban areas [1]							
Participation rate [2]	55.2	54.7	55.4	55.2	55.0	55.4	55.5
Unemployment rate	3.4	3.7	6.2	5.5	5.9	5.1	4.1
Unemployent rate (wider definition) [3]	5.6	6.1	8.6	6.4	6.9	5.8	5.0
Employment in small enterprises/total employment [4]	42.3	42.2	44.4	44.7	44.6	44.7	43.8
Uninsured wage earners/total wage earners	21.5	22.5	24.9	25.9	24.5	27.3	24.1
Part-time workers/total employment [5]	24.9	24.0	25.3	25.3	27.0	23.7	25.6

1. The *Encuesta Nacional de Empleo Urbano* covers a limited number of urban areas (initially 16, raised to 32 in 1992, and gradually thereafter to 43, as of 1997).
2. Labour force ("Economically active" population) as a percentage of population aged 12 year and over.
3. Open unemployment *plus* people who gave up seeking employment and are no longer included in the labour force but are available for work.
4. Small enterprises are defined as those with 1 to 5 employees.
5. Part-time workers are defined as those working less than 35 hours weekly.
Source: INEGI, *Encuesta Industrial Mensual, Estadistica de la Industria Maquiladora de Exportación, Encuesta Nacional de Empleo Urbano (ENEU)*; IMSS.

The urban unemployment rate (the best available indicator of "open" unemployment) has been declining continuously since its August 1995 peak (7.6 per cent) to 3.4 per cent in September 1997. The size of the turnaround – also noticeable for broader indicators of unemployment – is indicative of the reduction in labour market slack (Figure 4). However, the low level of the official unemployment rate does not provide an accurate indication of the structural under-utilisation of labour. The absence of unemployment insurance, combined with the very low income level of a large share of the population, is likely to limit the extent of open unemployment, so that the open unemployment rate can be thought of as the lower bound of unemployment, especially as rural areas are excluded from the surveys.[6]

Aggregate indicators suggest that the labour market adjusted rapidly through the crisis, but performance on a regional basis remained very uneven until the middle of 1997. In some states (in the North essentially), employment continued to expand during the 1995 recession (albeit at lower rates than in the previous year); in others, after a decline in 1995, it rebounded quickly to levels exceeding

Figure 4. **UNEMPLOYMENT IN URBAN AREAS**

As a percentage of labour force (12 years and over)

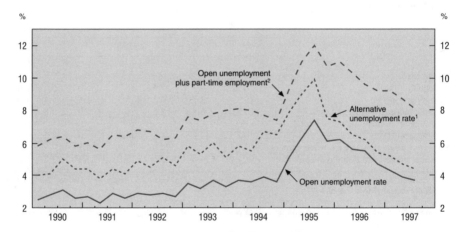

1. Includes those who stopped searching for a job but are still available for work.
2. Part-time refers to employees working less than 15 hours a week.
Source: INEGI.

those of 1994. Other states still (mainly in the South and the Federal District), where productive activities are predominantly oriented to the domestic market, have experienced a protracted decline in employment. Whereas in the aggregate, wage flexibility is likely to have cushioned the adjustment of employment in the recession and facilitated its rebound afterwards, this has not necessarily been the case on a regional basis, as several states – Chiapas, Guerrero, Morelos – suffered both the most severe job losses and drastic real wage cuts during the crisis. Nevertheless, by the first quarter of 1997, net job creation (on the basis of insured workers) was sufficient to bring the real wage bill in all the states above its level a year earlier, offsetting the impact of the contraction in real average earnings recorded in 1996, but still not matching pre-crisis levels.

Disinflation continues

The process of disinflation that started around mid-1995 continued in 1996 and 1997, with the year-on-year increase in the CPI falling below 20 per cent as from mid-1997, down from 31 per cent a year earlier. In a context of cautious monetary and fiscal policy, two factors have helped the decline in inflation over the past two years: the relative stability of the nominal exchange rate since the start of 1996 (with a modest 1.7 per cent depreciation between the first quarters of 1996 and 1997 and stability in the following months); and a steady reduction in inflation expectations, as mirrored in continued moderate wage developments and the gradual reduction in private sector inflation forecasts. Prices of administratively-set goods and services (gasoline, electricity, natural gas ...) were raised in steps over the past two years, and the minimum wage was adjusted upward, as part of the measures agreed upon in the social pacts for 1996 and 1997.[7] These adjustments were reflected in short-term upward movements in the monthly inflation rate. The prices of some agricultural products were pushed upward as a result of the severe drought in the early months of 1996 (a supply shock to the 1996 CPI inflation rate equivalent to 2 percentage points according to estimates by the Bank of Mexico). Notwithstanding these short-term movements, by mid-1997 the monthly inflation rate had fallen below 1 per cent, from 1.5 per cent in June-July 1996.

In 1996, domestic prices of tradables continued to be boosted by the depreciation of the exchange rate, although the pass-through is likely to have been dampened by the depressed domestic market. Prices of non-tradable on the other hand (which account for 48.2 per cent of the CPI and are largely determined by labour costs) have been lagging behind those of tradable since the onset of the crisis, reflecting still weak domestic activity and moderate wage increases. The pattern changed in the early months of 1997, as increases in the prices of tradable fell below those of non-tradable, reflecting the disinflationary effect of real exchange rate appreciation.

For the second consecutive year, real wages declined throughout 1996 – by an average 11 per cent, on the basis of earnings in manufacturing, following a 12 per cent decline in 1995. In the first half of 1997, the real wage reduction became smaller. Real compensation of employees in manufacturing stopped falling in the middle of 1997, and wage increases negotiated around that period – at about 20 per cent – were, for the first time since the onset of the crisis, as high (or higher) than the current rate of inflation. Contractual wages, which are negotiated at the firm level, suffered the largest real cut in 1995 (16.8 per cent on average) as a result of the unanticipated surge of inflation, and a more limited one in 1996 (4.2 per cent); this pattern reflects the collective agreement process for unionised workers, which does not allow for a revision of the contracts in the 12-month period following the settlement. Given the degree of labour market slack, contracts have tended to be negotiated on the basis of lower inflation expected over the forthcoming year, with no catch-up on losses accumulated since the start of the crisis. In the context of the social pacts, the minimum wage increased by a cumulative 23.4 per cent from November 1995 to November 1996 (2 percentage points more than initially programmed), and 17 per cent in December 1996, as set in the Pact for 1997 in accordance with the inflation target 12 months ahead. This implies a further decline in its purchasing power, although, since the onset of the 1994/95 peso crisis, cumulated reductions in the real minimum wage have been smaller than those for average real earnings (Figure 5, Panel A).

Within manufacturing, the *maquiladora* sector recorded smaller real wage cuts than the rest of the economy, reflecting strong output growth and high productivity gains. The construction sector, on the other hand, suffered the most dramatic cuts in real wages (by a cumulative 32 per cent over the two years, of which more than half occurred in 1996). These real wage adjustments facilitated a recovery in net job creation exceeding output growth (based on survey data for

Figure 5. **REAL WAGES, LABOUR PRODUCTIVITY AND PRICE TRENDS**

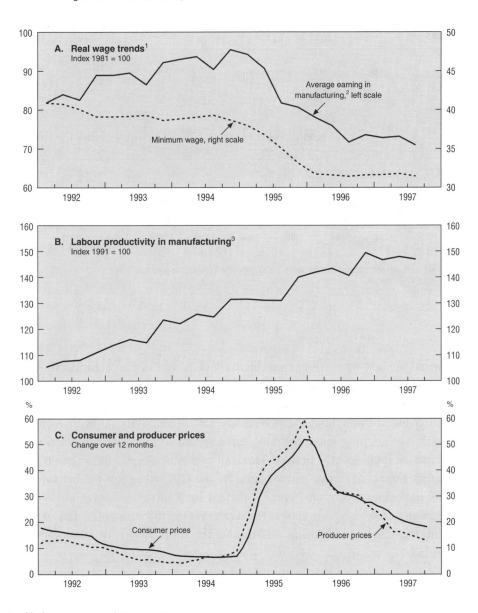

1. Moving average over three quarters.
2. Wages, salaries and social benefits, based on INEGI monthly industrial survey.
3. Real output per man-hour, moving average over three quarters.
Source: INEGI and Banco de México.

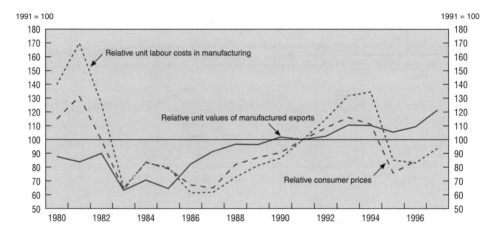

Figure 6. **MEXICO'S RELATIVE COMPETITIVE POSITION**

Indices in US$ terms

Note: 1997 data are estimates; a fall indicates improvement in competitive position.
Source: OECD estimates.

the formal sector), with average productivity of labour in the sector declining. In manufacturing, on the other hand, labour productivity rose sharply with the recovery of output in 1996 and the first half of 1997, and employment in the sector expanded throughout the period. Overall productivity gains, in combination with the on-going wage restraint, have served to moderate the deterioration in international competitiveness of Mexican products, despite the strength of the real effective exchange rate as measured by the CPI. Although the behaviour of various indicators of competitiveness differs markedly, the appreciation of the real exchange rate does not appear to have reversed the substantial fall of 1995, particularly when considering relative unit labour costs in manufacturing (Figure 6).

Normalisation of the external position

With the abrupt reversal of net foreign capital flows in December 1994 and the severe stabilisation policies that followed, the current account deficit shrank

Table 5.

Table 5. **Balance of payments, current account**

US$ billion, annualised

	1994	1995	1996	1996 S1	1996 S2	1997 S1
Exports, f.o.b.[1]	60.9	79.5	96.0	91.0	101.0	104.8
Imports, f.o.b.[1]	79.3	72.5	89.5	82.7	96.2	100.7
Trade balance	**−18.5**	**7.1**	**6.5**	**8.3**	**4.8**	**4.2**
(% GDP)	(-4.4)	(2.5)	(2.0)	(2.6)	(1.4)	(1.1)
of which: Maquiladoras	5.8	4.9	6.4	5.8	7.0	7.9
Non factor services, net	−2.0	0.7	0.5	1.4	−0.3	0.6
of which: Tourism	1.0	3.0	3.5	4.2	2.9	4.6
Investment income, net	−13.0	−13.3	−13.5	−13.2	−13.8	−12.7
Transfers, net	3.8	4.0	4.5	4.5	4.6	4.7
Current account balance	**−29.7**	**−1.6**	**−1.9**	**0.9**	**−4.7**	**−3.3**
(% GDP)	(-7.0)	(-0.6)	(-0.6)	(0.3)	(-1.3)	(-0.9)

1. Including trade by in-bond industries.
Source: Banco de México.

to 0.5 per cent of GDP in 1995 (from 7 per cent of GDP in 1994). It remained around that level in 1996, as renewed capital inflows were used to repay debt incurred under the financial assistance package and to restore international reserves. But there was a widening of the current account in the course of the year and into 1997, closely related to trends in the merchandise trade balance, while the balance on services and transfers has been relatively stable (Table 5). The trade account posted a surplus of about the same size in 1995 and 1996 – US$7.1 and 6.5 billion, respectively – compared with the 1994 US$18.5 billion deficit (Figure 7). However trade patterns changed significantly between 1995 and 1996. Exports continued to grow in 1996, while imports, which had been falling to mid-1995, picked up following the recovery of domestic demand. This pattern continued in 1997, against a background of expanding net capital inflows from abroad. As a result, the trade surplus in January-October 1997 had shrunk to US$1.6 billion against US$5.8 billion in the same period a year earlier.

Trade flows and the current account

Although export growth slowed gradually as domestic markets were regaining strength, by 1997 the level of merchandise exports was about 80 per cent

Figure 7. **FOREIGN TRADE, CURRENT ACCOUNT AND EXPORT PERFORMANCE**

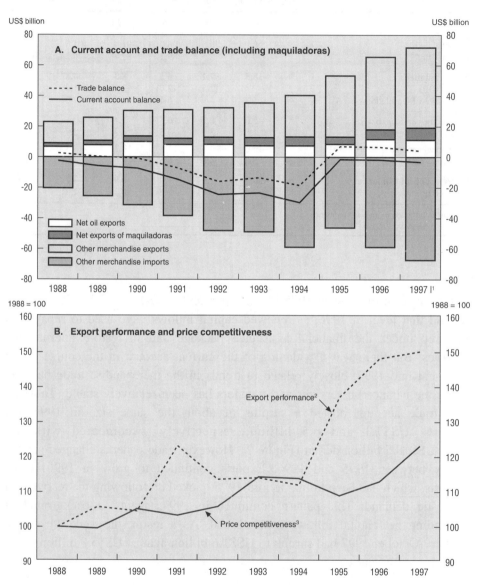

1. Annualised figures.
2. Ratio of Mexico's exports of manufactures to its main partners imports of manufactures in volume terms.
3. Relative export unit value of manufactured goods. A rise indicates a deterioration.
Source: OECD estimates and Banco de México.

above the 1994 level (based on data over 10 months in dollar terms). The current pace of expansion (15 per cent, year-on-year, in January-October 1997) applies to a much larger base than three years ago. Oil exports were boosted in 1996 as a result of higher world oil prices and a 20 per cent volume increase, reaching US$11.7 billion, the highest level in 10 years. In January-October 1997, they remained close to the level a year earlier as oil prices remained broadly unchanged. Manufacturing exports (currently 85 per cent of total merchandise exports) have been the most dynamic component of exports with the expansion driven by the machinery and transport equipment sub-sector, most notably auto-motive exports. The *maquiladora* export industry, concentrated in major cities along the northern border area, remains a driving force for regional development and employment creation (accounting for one-third of jobs created in manufactur-ing in 1996, and more than 80 per cent in some states), but integration of domestic industries with the *maquiladoras* remains low, as the latter rely heavily upon foreign inputs. Exports by non-*maquiladoras*, which were expanding more rapidly than those of the *maquiladora* sector in 1995 and 1996, have lost some momentum in 1997 as domestic demand strengthened.[8]

With the recovery of consumption and investment at the start of 1996, imports for these categories of goods picked up after declining in 1995. At the same time imports of intermediate inputs (by far the larger component), which had continued to grow during the slump to feed exporting industries, gained momentum. In 1997, imports of both consumption and investment goods expanded at rates above 37 per cent from a year earlier, but in the case of consumption goods this did not suffice to return to 1994 levels. Imports of capital goods, on the other hand, exceeded 1994 levels. While purchases of these goods by export enterprises continued to grow rapidly, those of other companies expanded at a faster pace (42 per cent) – a sign of more favourable growth prospects for domestic activities.

The on-going gradual narrowing of the trade surplus reflects essentially changes in volumes (comparing the first nine months of 1997 with the same period a year earlier).[9] Terms of trade changes remained very small, because Mexico is by and large a price taker in international trade. Other factors contrib-uted to the outcome: first, the exchange rate remained broadly unchanged until October 1997; second, a large part of exports is priced in dollars, not only in the case of oil, but also for manufacturing goods produced by foreign companies for export (*e.g.* automobiles); third, the price of oil, despite a decline in the first months of 1997, is close to its level at the start of 1996. Mexico's strong export performance in 1996 and 1997, measured as the volume growth in manufactures exports less growth of foreign markets, shows that some of the gains in market shares achieved in 1995 in response to a slump in domestic demand are of a durable nature, as a result of the modernisation and increased capacity of exporting industries.

Non-factor services posted a small surplus in 1996, just below that recorded in 1995, as increased net revenue from tourism was offset by higher import-related payments on freight and insurance.[10] In the first half of 1997, the non-factor service account was close to balance. The deficit on net investment income remained broadly unchanged in 1996, at 13.5 billion, as the decline in interest paid by the public sector on its foreign debt was offset by an increase in private sector interest payments and by higher profits on foreign direct investment (FDI). In the first half of 1997, net interest payments fell slightly from their level a year earlier, reflecting reduced external debt of the public sector and lower interest rates both abroad and domestically.[11] An additional factor in the reduction of the deficit on investment income has been the higher revenue from interest payments on foreign debt held by Mexican residents. At the same time, profits on FDI continued to increase. Gross interest payments – reaching 12.4 billion in 1997I (annualised) – heavily dominate payments of factor services, but in future years, given the scale of cumulated FDI over the recent past, profits on foreign direct investment – 4.2 billion, on an annual basis in 1997I compared with 2.5 billion in the early 1990s – will weigh increasingly on payments of factor services. Workers' remittances, which make up most of transfer revenue, have grown steadily since the onset of the crisis, in line with trends in previous years.

Capital transactions

The capital account recorded a US$11.3 surplus in 1996, excluding operations carried out under the international financial assistance package, compared with a deficit of approximately the same size in 1995 on the same basis (*i.e.* considering market-determined flows only). This recovery of net inflows in 1996 and the first half of 1997 has been driven by foreign investors' improved confidence in the Mexican economy (notwithstanding some uncertainty linked to the mid-1997 elections). Foreign investment on the stock and bond markets soared in

1996 and the first half of 1997, particularly in securities issued by the public sector in foreign currency. Foreign direct investment (FDI) in 1996 declined slightly from the very high 1995 level; but in the first half of 1997 it reached US$ 4 billion, on a half-yearly basis, suggesting that the total for the year is likely to be above the 1996 outcome.[12] Whereas in 1996I FDI almost matched portfolio investment, in the first half of 1997 the situation seems to have changed with portfolio investment greatly exceeding FDI. The regained confidence has allowed a pick-up in interest-sensitive inflows, mostly long-term (private sector securities issued abroad and foreigners' purchases of domestic stocks and bonds). In 1997I, of a total of US$12.7 billion of net foreign investment, only US$0.3 billion were acquisitions of short-term paper in the money market. FDI has continued to be predominantly directed towards the industrial sector, although foreign investment

Table 6. **Balance of payments, capital account**

US$ billion, annualised

	1994	1995	1996	1996 S1	1996 S2	1997 S1
Capital account	**14.6**	**15.4**	**3.3**	**0.3**	**6.3**	**9.8**
Liabilities	**20.3**	**22.8**	**9.8**	**4.8**	**14.8**	**9.4**
Loans and deposits	1.1	23.0	−12.0	−9.4	−14.5	−16.1
Public sector	−0.4	11.5	−8.9	−5.3	−12.5	−9.4
Development banks	1.3	1.0	−1.2	−3.7	1.3	−1.5
Non-financial public sector	−1.7	10.5	−7.7	−1.6	−13.8	−7.9
Bank of Mexico	−1.2	13.3	−3.5	−4.0	−3.1	−6.4
Commercial banks	1.5	−5.0	1.5	−2.1	−0.9	−5.5
Non-financial private sector	1.2	3.1	2.0	2.0	2.0	5.1
Total foreign investments	19.2	−0.2	21.8	14.2	29.3	25.4
Direct investment	11.0	9.5	7.6	6.4	8.8	7.9
Portfolio investment	8.2	−9.7	14.2	7.8	20.5	17.6
of which:						
Stock market	4.1	0.5	3.0	3.8	2.2	4.7
Money market	−2.2	−13.9	0.9	−1.5	3.3	0.6
Assets	**−5.7**	**−7.4**	**−6.5**	**−4.5**	**−8.4**	**0.5**
In foreign banks	−3.7	−3.2	−6.2	−5.9	−6.5	1.8
Credits to non-residents	0.0	−0.3	−0.6	−0.6	−0.6	−0.5
External debt garantees	−0.6	−0.7	0.5	0.8	0.2	−0.7
Other	−1.3	−3.2	−0.2	1.2	−1.6	−0.2
Errors and omissions	−3.3	−4.2	0.4	−1.9	2.6	2.0
Changes in reserves (increase = −)	**18.4**	**−9.6**	**−1.8**	**0.7**	**−4.2**	**−8.4**

Source: Banco de México.

in the service sector increased considerably in recent years (now accounting for one-third of the stock of FDI, with industry's share having fallen to about half). Recent developments suggest that, in Mexico, FDI has tended to be relatively isolated from domestic market performance:[13] It has been predominantly directed to export-oriented activities, rather than aiming at selling to the domestic market. This relative insensitivity to local conditions served to partly offset swings in the domestic component of gross fixed capital formation during the current cycle.

If operations related to the international rescue package are included, the capital account posted a US$15.4 billion surplus in 1995 – reflecting borrowing by the Bank of Mexico and the public sector to repay dollar-linked securities (*Tesobonos*) to foreign holders, and to rebuild foreign reserves. In 1996, the capital account surplus declined to US$3.3 billion, as a result of substantial loan repayments (Table 6). Increased foreign liquidity allowed the Bank of Mexico and the Federal government to pay in advance a portion of the outstanding balance of the international assistance. Loans and deposits moved from a US$23 billion inflow in 1995 to a 12 billion outflow in 1996, reflecting net payments to monetary authorities of the US and Canada and to multilateral institutions (IMF, IDB and World Bank). In the first half of 1997, similar operations took place, with the advance repayment of the US$3.5 billion out-standing debt to the US Treasury, while 2.7 billion were paid to the IMF. With strong capital inflows and a moderate current account deficit, international reserves were built up and by October 1997, they amounted to over US$25 billion.

The short-term outlook

National accounts for the first three-quarters of 1997 point to a quickening of economic growth and a broadening of its base. Given the strengthening of business and household confidence and their improved cash-flow, combined with the reduction in nominal and real interest rates, GDP is likely to continue to expand at a rapid pace. The neutral stance of monetary policy, in combination with new public investment projects that are to come on stream, creates an environment supportive of output growth over the short term. Real GDP growth, estimated to average close to 7 per cent in 1997, is projected to slow somewhat in 1998, as the process of catching up from the dramatically low levels of domestic demand reached in 1995 comes to completion. The Secretariat's projections rely upon the following main assumptions:

- in accordance with the usual technical assumptions underlying the OECD Secretariat's projections, the nominal exchange rate is unchanged over the projection period (at 8.24 pesos to a dollar, the rate prevailing on 3 November 1997);
- the average dollar price of internationally traded oil is assumed to decline to US$18.5/bb in the second half of 1997 and average US$18.3 in 1998 (US$2.3 below the 1996 peak) the average export price of Mexican oil, though at a lower level, is assumed to decline in parallel;
- Mexico's manufactures export markets are estimated to grow by 12 per cent in 1998, a marked deceleration from the increase in 1997, largely due to the expected slowdown of activity in North America;
- a small demand stimulus is expected from the assumed reduction in the primary budget surplus of the public sector in 1998;
- short-term interest rates are expected to continue to come down over the projection horizon, in line with Bank of Mexico announced policy, to reflect the decline in inflation and a gradual reduction in the risk premium (for details on announced policies, see chapter II below).

In the near term, the recovery in real wages bodes well for a strengthening of private consumption, as the recovery is spreading more evenly across income categories, boosting purchases of a wider range of consumer goods. Improved cash-flow of households and a backlog in demand should induce a rebound of residential construction, albeit from very low levels.[14] Infrastructure investment will continue to support construction activity. Growth in machinery and equipment purchases is expected to slow down somewhat, from the record rates reached during the 1996-97 recovery: by 1998, the ratio of gross fixed capital formation to GDP should reach 20 per cent (at constant prices), slightly exceeding the pre-crisis ratio. All in all, the contribution to GDP growth from consumption and from investment is expected to be more balanced than in the initial phase of the recovery (Table 7). With the expected steady decline in nominal and real interests rates and the revival of domestic activity now underway, growth is likely to be more evenly spread across sectors and regions; but catching up of the most depressed regions is likely to be a slow process.

Table 7. **Short-term projections**

	1995	1996	1997[1]	1998[1]
	Percentage changes			
Demand and output (volume)[2]				
Private consumption	−9.5	2.3	5.0	4.4
Public consumption	−1.3	3.7	4.2	3.2
Gross fixed capital formation	−29.0	17.7	19.2	15.4
Final domestic demand	−12.3	4.8	7.3	6.4
Change in stockbuilding[3]	−2.1	1.6	1.1	0.2
Total domestic demand	**−13.9**	**6.5**	**8.3**	**6.4**
Exports of goods and services	33.0	18.7	16.0	12.5
Imports of goods and services	−12.8	27.8	23.0	16.2
Change in foreign balance[3]	8.5	−1.2	−1.4	−0.9
GDP at market prices	**−6.2**	**5.1**	**6.7**	**5.4**
Inflation (average)				
GDP deflator	38.0	31.5	19.5	13.0
Private consumption deflator	34.0	34.0	20.9	13.7
	Levels			
Current account balance				
Per cent of GDP	−0.5	−0.6	−1.6	−2.7
US$ billion	−1.6	−1.9	−6.5	−12.4

1. OECD estimates for 1997, projections for 1998.
2. At 1993 constant prices.
3. As a percentage of previous year's GDP.
Source: OECD estimates and projections.

The trade balance is likely to post a deficit in the later part of 1997. Two opposing forces will be at play over the projection period: as the real exchange rate appreciates (under the technical assumption of the OECD Secretariat of fixed nominal exchange rates) price competitiveness is likely to deteriorate; the scale of the deterioration is difficult to assess in view of the different signals provided by various indicators. On the other hand, the expansion of the export base achieved in 1996 suggests that non-price competitiveness factors – enhanced marketing efforts, wider and more modern export capacity – are likely to continue to play a role. Under the Secretariat's projections for 1998, Mexican exporters achieve further gains in market shares. With sustained import growth, however, the trade account deficit is expected to widen gradually over the projection horizon. The deficit on factor services is expected to increase between 1997 and 1998, as a result of higher interest payments on the private external debt and larger profit repatriation, only partly offset by an increase in workers' remittances. These elements combined will translate into a widening of the current account deficit equivalent to 1 percentage point of GDP – from an estimated US$6.5 billion in 1997 to just above 12 billion in 1998 (around 2½ per cent of GDP) according to the Secretariat's projections.

Continuing improvement on the labour market is expected with the broadening of the recovery of economic activity. As more jobs are generated in the "formal" economy, in particular in the formal segment of construction and the service sector, labour is expected to shift from informal activities into insured and better-remunerated occupations. This shift will be reflected in an increasing number of workers insured by IMSS. The urban unemployment rate is expected to stabilise close to its low pre-crisis level, but given the overall labour market slack (*i.e.* low-productivity employment in the service sector and in rural areas), average earnings are expected to remain moderate over the projection period; in addition sustained productivity gains should continue to keep a lid on unit labour costs. Inflation is projected to continue to come down, reaching 12 per cent by December 1998 year-on-year (implying an average annual inflation rate of about 13½ per cent, based on the private consumption deflator).

Some of the risks attached to the projections are associated with the over-indebtedness of the private sector and the banks' precarious financial situation. Although the banking sector's situation has improved, its soundness hasn't been fully restored (see Part III below). Banks and debtors remain quite vulnerable to movements in interest rates; and a steady decline in nominal and real interest rates is key to the unravelling of problems. The size and the nature of capital flows are uncertain; upward pressures on the exchange rate may appear as a result of large capital inflows associated with the strengthening of confidence. Despite a steady real appreciation of the peso since the massive 1994/95 devaluation, the widening current account deficit does not appear to reflect losses in cost-competitiveness of Mexican exports. Over a longer horizon, as recognised in the government's medium-term programme, rapid growth of output and employment requires a high level of fixed investment (see last section in Part II below). Unless domestic saving is strengthened, this would carry the risk of relying heavily on borrowing from abroad, making the economy vulnerable to sudden shifts in foreign investors' confidence, especially if capital inflows are short-term.

II. Economic policies

Introduction

The focus of economic policy has shifted from immediate crisis management in 1995 towards fostering the recovery in 1996-97; and it now faces the challenge of ensuring the transition to sustainable balanced growth over the medium term. Within this overall setting, the monetary programmes for 1996 and 1997 have focused on gradual disinflation and stabilisation of financial markets. Fiscal policy has remained cautious in 1996 and 1997, maintaining a broadly balanced budget, and securing a continuous decline in the public debt/GDP ratio. Avoiding a build-up of macroeconomic imbalances and the periodic crises that have plagued Mexico in the past is a central policy concern. In this context, the need for policy makers to formulate an explicit medium-term framework became increasingly clear. As noted in past OECD Surveys, this framework could serve to guide private sector expectations and to provide a benchmark against which to measure policy performance; the government's National Programme for Financing Development, 1997-2000 (PRONAFIDE), presented in June 1997, aims to fill this role. The present chapter first discusses monetary policy and financial market developments, with particular emphasis on the monetary policy framework that has developed since the crisis. This is followed by a review of fiscal policy. The last section of the chapter provides an overview and summary appraisal of the medium-term macro-economic scenario, PRONAFIDE.

Monetary policy and financial market developments

In the aftermath of the 1994-95 crisis, a new monetary policy framework was established in pursuit of the key objectives of containing inflation and stabilising financial markets. The build-up of confidence in this new framework has played an important role in the normalisation of market conditions, facilitating the decline in real interest rates and a recovery in economic activity. The disinflation path announced in PRONAFIDE plays a role as an anchor for medium-term inflation expectations. A further enhancement of the monetary policy framework would be the confirmation of the central bank's long-term objective of price stability,[15] as well as regularly scheduled assessments of the inflation outlook over the medium term and clear indications of how the Bank intends to accomplish its targets. Such an enhancement would provide guidance for future price expectations and facilitate the attainment of the long-term objective of price stability. Against this background, an immediate issue confronting monetary authorities is to choose the pace at which the long-term price stability objective should be approached.

The monetary policy framework

The present policy framework has developed both as a result of the move to central bank independence in 1994 and in response to events as the 1995 crisis unfolded. A gradual lifting of the rigid exchange rate anchor had already taken place between 1990 and 1994.[16] The remaining constraints on exchange rate flexibility were abandoned at the end of 1994, when the fluctuation band proved insufficient to accommodate the loss of confidence in the peso. Under the new framework there is no central bank commitment to the level of the exchange rate. The legislation that made the central bank independent also increased its accountability. The Bank is bound by a Constitutional mandate to aim at price stability, and in its annual policy statement (issued in January) it must explain to Congress how it intends to pursue this objective. The first such policy document was produced in 1995, when the shift to a policy of free floating created the need to provide the market with new signals and credible commitments. The main features of the central bank's annual monetary programme are the announcement of an annual inflation objective and the use of the monetary base as an intermediate target. In that context, the Bank has also announced an annual ceiling on its domestic credit expansion as part of its policy commitments. The role of this ceiling has been to make pursuit of the intermediate target for base money contingent on a minimum increase in international reserves. In the present system, intermediate targets for monetary aggregates play a more conspicuous role than they do in other countries pursuing explicit inflation-targets.

Instruments and targets

Since 1995, the central bank has announced an annual target for inflation – on the basis of the December-to-December growth rate of the CPI – and the time path of the monetary base used as an intermediate target. The yearly inflation target has been at the core of a policy that aims at a gradual reduction of inflation in order to reach the long-term price stability objective. The inflation target is determined jointly by the central bank and the Finance Ministry in order to ensure consistency in the general macroeconomic policy framework. The intermediate monetary base target is set by the central bank in accordance with the inflation target, as well as output growth and interest rate projections.

The daily liquidity management system is the vehicle for making the Bank's strategy operational. The Bank does not exogenously fix the supply of base money,[17] in fact it accommodates the demand for cash by providing the banking system with the liquidity it requires on any day. But the Bank can – and does – induce changes in the money market by altering the terms on which the required liquidity is provided. The amount of liquidity provided by the Bank on any day through operations in money markets may exceed or fall short of the liquidity requirements of banks. When commercial banks face a surplus or a shortfall in cash, they credit or debit their accounts with the central bank. The system, by design, provides incentives to the banks to keep a zero average balance on their central bank account.[18] The central bank uses the announcement that the overall position of the banks will be a surplus (*i.e.* "long") or an overdraft (*i.e.* "short") as a signal to clarify policy intentions and induce changes in money market conditions. The announcement of a "short" position – *i.e.* that the banking system as a whole will be in overdraft – induces market participants to bid up interest rates in an attempt to avoid payment of the overdraft rate at the central bank. Likewise, announcement of a "long" position induces a fall in interest rates. By using this signal, the central bank can bring about adjustment in money market conditions without having to become a market maker (*i.e.* setting interest rates).

The Bank avoids predetermining the exchange rate or providing signals regarding desired levels of the exchange rate. Nonetheless, it has followed a policy of gradual reserve accumulation and its policy framework does include a number of features aimed at reducing exchange rate volatility and uncertainties that may heighten perceptions of exchange rate risk. Firstly, the Bank is committed to limit the use of domestic credit expansion (mostly consisting of central bank purchases of government paper and credit to the banking system) as a source of base money creation. Secondly, the Bank specifies a minimum target for foreign reserve accumulation. In essence, these twin commitments imply that

---

Box 1.   The central bank's foreign exchange transactions

Since August 1996, the Bank has used an innovative procedure for reserve acquisition which does not predetermine the exchange rate and should reduce market volatility by limiting the pace of appreciation.[1] Under this mechanism, the Bank sells contracts (put-options) that carry the commitment to purchase a certain amount of foreign exchange. The purchase price would be either the exchange rate of the day previous to that in which the option is exercised by its holder, or the average exchange rate of the preceding 20 business days if the market exchange rate exceeds this average. A predetermined quantity of these put-options are sold by auction each month.[2] The price that buyers are willing to pay for the option is an indicator of their expectations regarding future peso appreciation. The foreign exchange options provide a transparent mechanism to acquire international reserves at precisely those moments when the exchange rate is strongest, as the options will be exercised when appreciation pressures develop.

In February 1997, a second mechanism was put in place to limit exchange rate volatility by reducing the risk of an abrupt depreciation. Under this mechanism, every business day the Bank auctions a pre-announced quantity of foreign exchange (currently US$200 million) at an asking price 2 per cent above the market rate observed on the previous business day. Thus market participants will only offer bids when the exchange rate has depreciated by more than 2 per cent on that day. This second auction mechanism provides a guarantee that, even under conditions of uncertainty, the market will remain sufficiently liquid so as to avoid situations under which even small-scale trading can cause disproportionate moves in market rates. Here again, the policy framework seeks to maintain orderly foreign exchange market conditions without commitment to a specific exchange rate value.

---

1. This mechanism was introduced by a decision of the Foreign Exchange Commission, the authority responsible for setting exchange rate policy. Both the Ministry of Finance and the Bank of Mexico are represented in the Commission. The resolutions of the Commission require a favourable vote of at least one representative of the Ministry of Finance.

2. On 17 February 1997, the Exchange Commission decided that if 80 per cent or more of the dollar options auctioned for any given month were to be exercised before the 16th of the month, the Bank of Mexico would call for a new auction. Banks could exercise their rights under this additional auction only during the remaining time of the corresponding month.

the intermediate target for base money growth is conditional on a satisfactory balance-of-payments outcome: lower monetary growth would result if balance-of-payments developments were to fall short of the implied threshold. Thirdly, the Bank does not act as a price setter in money markets, a move that increases the role of interest rates in absorbing shocks to liquidity and reduces the volatility of the exchange rate. Finally, the Bank's foreign exchange transactions are constrained to operations with the public sector and to purchases/sales from the market through a transparent mechanism that does not pre-determine the level of the exchange rate (see Box 1).

The 1996 and 1997 monetary programmes

In 1996, despite slippage by 7 percentage points from the official target of 20.5 per cent, a clear downward trend was established as inflation dropped from 52 per cent in 1995 to 27.7 per cent (Table 8). The policy announcement for 1997, by setting the target at 15 per cent, reaffirmed this clear downward path for inflation. A second objective guiding central bank operations has been to maintain orderly market conditions in the foreign exchange and money markets. In its mid-term policy review of September, in view of favourable developments on the inflation front and reduced uncertainty, the Bank announced changes to its operating procedures including measures to deal with surges in short-term capital inflows.

Table 8.   **Monetary programmes, 1996-97: targets and outcomes**

	1996		1997
	Target	Outcome	Target
Inflation target December to December (per cent)	20.5	27.7	15.0
Change in Monetary base			
Million pesos	18 000	17 182	20 580
Per cent	27.0	24.5	24.5
Ceiling on change in NDC[1] (million pesos)	7 220	−28 260	−745
Minimum change in net foreign assets (US$ million)	1 400	5 864	2 500
Memorandum items (per cent change):			
Real GDP	3.0	5.1	4.5
Nominal GDP	38.1	38.4	24.8

1.   Net domestic credit.
Source: Banco de México.

1996 outcomes

In 1996, an intermediate target for base money was set in line with the GDP growth and inflation assumptions of the government's November budget document. On the basis of the Bank's empirical estimates of money demand, the expansion in demand for base money was to be slightly larger than nominal GDP growth as the decline in inflation and falling interest rates were to lead to "re-monetisation" of the economy during the year. To meet the expected increase in the demand for base money, the Bank set as an intermediate target for base money supply an increase of some 27 per cent (*i.e.* 18 billion pesos) relative to its end-1995 level.

Base money growth was marginally weaker than intended, despite higher-than-targeted inflation and output growth in excess of initial expectations because re-monetisation failed to take place. Base money growth came about exclusively from accumulation of net foreign assets as domestic credit contracted in absolute terms.[19] In real terms, the monetary base shrank by 1.6 per cent relative to its level at end-1995, as several factors acted to induce a smaller demand for base money, one of which being the greater use of debit cards. More fundamental was the considerable slack in labour markets: demand for base money is strongly influenced by the income of wage earners,[20] and real wages declined again in 1996.

Trends in 1997

The monetary programme for 1997 established a base money growth target of 24.5 per cent (an increase of some 20.6 billion pesos). This intermediate target was deemed consistent with the official inflation target of 15 per cent and a 4.5 per cent estimate for real output growth.[21] The Bank's 1997 monetary programme provided for growth in base money demand to be 3.6 percentage points above projected growth in nominal GDP. The implied re-monetisation process would be in line with sustained disinflation and a continued downward trend in nominal interest rates. Furthermore, the fact that re-monetisation did not take place in 1996 might have been due to adjustment lags, rather than to a permanent decline in the base money to GDP ratio.

During the first half of 1997, the Bank followed what it defines as a "neutral" policy stance by passively accommodating all shifts in base money demand; it did not create any net debtor ("short") or net creditor ("long") positions for the banking system *vis-à-vis* the central bank. In its January policy document the Bank had committed itself not to use "long" positions – an announcement that was intended to calm potential fears of policy relaxation in the lead-up to the July parliamentary elections. The Bank did not make use of "short" positions either, as inflation developments remained in line with the monetary programme. During the first four months of 1997, the monetary base was broadly in line with the annual target, once account is taken of seasonal patterns. Base money growth was kept close to target by means of further contraction in net domestic credit of the central bank, combined with continued accumulation of foreign reserves. By June 1997, net international assets[22] amounted to US$14.3 billion, up nearly US$8 billion since end-1996, a figure that compares with the minimum increase of US$2.5 billion stated in the programme for the year as a whole. The Bank's net domestic credit, defined as the difference between monetary base and net international assets, recorded a decline of 67.3 billion pesos during the first semester.

In the second quarter of 1997, however, base money began to deviate from the Bank's daily announced target, a development that continued into the third quarter (Figure 8). It may point to stronger than expected growth in money demand, induced by higher than expected real income growth and a more pronounced decline in nominal interest rates than anticipated. There are also signs of a broader pickup in deposit taking activities of banks, which has lifted the demand deposit component of M1, and this may signal a recovery in demand for transactions instruments.

Deviations from the intermediate target for base money can pose communication difficulties for the Bank. The Bank's announced rule is that deviations of outcomes from (intermediate) targets for base money will be corrected if they are inconsistent with achieving the inflation target. Thus, deviations from target are acceptable to the extent that they reflect stronger growth in real money demand, traceable to deviations from the expected path of real GDP growth or of the speed of the re-monetisation process. While the rule is clear-cut, its implementation raises several issues, as the pace of the recovery and that of the re-monetisation process remain difficult to predict and can be observed only with a lag. In this context, the monetary authorities have felt the need to keep markets informed regarding the economic outlook and the considerations underlying liquidity management. In its September mid-term policy report, the Bank confirmed that it did

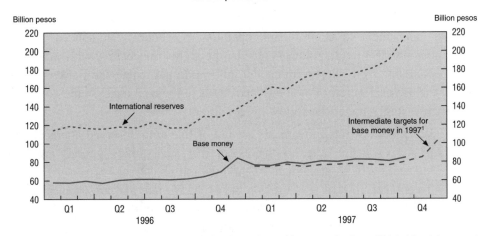

Figure 8. **RECENT EVOLUTION IN BASE MONEY
AND IN INTERNATIONAL ASSETS OF THE CENTRAL BANK**
End of period balances

1. The acceleration of base money at the end of each year is a stable seasonal pattern which is taken into account in the central bank's target definition.
Source: Banco de México.

consider the observed deviation from the original base money target as an acceptable outcome due to shifts in real money demand and consistent with attainment of the inflation target. So far, the deviation of base money growth from initial targets has not brought about any adverse reaction in interest rates, probably because inflation developments have continued to be favourable.

The strong growth in international reserves has not caused conflicts in the control of monetary aggregates, mainly because the central bank still has an unsatisfied demand for reserve accumulation. However, such accumulation of reserves is not without cost, and the central bank may be approaching the point at which questions arise regarding the burden associated with further reserve accumulation. So far, authorities view a higher level of reserves as advantageous since it has a favourable influence on the terms and conditions under which the country has access to international capital markets. However, the appropriate level of reserves is likely to be lower now than in the past as a result of the move to a floating exchange rate system and improved access to international capital markets for many Mexican borrowers. Reflecting these considerations, the

43

Exchange Commission, in September 1997 and again in October, reduced the amount of foreign exchange the Bank may potentially acquire through the options mechanism.

An adjustment to central bank operating procedures, announced in the September policy report, points to greater flexibility in dealing with potential pressures arising from short-term capital inflows. In particular, the Bank will re-instate the use of net creditor (''long'') positions of the banking system – a signal of policy easing – under the following conditions:

- When interest rate movements are out of line with observed appreciation of the exchange rate, to the extent that such policy actions are not inconsistent with attainment of the inflation objective.
- To counter upward pressures on the exchange rate that are unsustainable and linked solely to shifts in short-term capital inflows.
- To re-establish orderly market conditions in domestic money markets.
- When there are clear and well-founded reasons to believe that inflation in the period ahead is most likely to fall below its announced target.

The policy announcement reflects the favourable development of inflation in the previous months and the lifting of uncertainties that prevailed in the first semester of 1997. It also reveals the authorities' concern that surges in short-term capital inflows may engender exchange rate misalignment. Uncertainties regarding US monetary policy and the risk of an adverse market reaction in the wake of the mid-term July elections may have moderated the scope for reducing interest rates during the first half of 1997. In the event, US long-term interest rates declined and Mexican debt and equity markets recorded further gains in the third quarter. Up to October 1997, the exchange rate also remained strong, despite successive increases in the size of the foreign exchange options mechanism (see Box 1). Near the end of October, Mexican financial markets were hit by the chain reaction spreading from Southeast Asia to stock and exchange markets around the world. The effects on Mexican markets have been, nevertheless, subdued. By the first week of November, the bilateral peso/dollar exchange rate had depreci-ated to 8.2 pesos per dollar and the 3-month Cetes rate had risen again above 20 per cent. In the future, the greater flexibility introduced into monetary policy should allow the Bank to absorb pressure from short-term capital inflows by a combination of interest rate and exchange rate changes without departing from its stated inflation objective.

Financial market developments since 1996

Monetary and credit aggregates

A recovery in demand for bank deposits started during the first half of 1996, and by mid-year annual growth rates for real financial saving had turned positive (Figure 9). So far, increased financial saving has not translated into a pickup in credit to the private sector. The balance of credit outstanding to the private sector still recorded negative real growth rates in the first semester of 1997, even though the rate of decline was less pronounced (Table 9). At the same time, given the government's balanced accounts, there has been very little pressure on overall domestic financing requirements. This combination left banks with ample liquidity, which they used in 1996 to repay foreign liabilities, a process that seems to have continued in 1997.

Several factors have impeded a more rapid normalisation of credit market conditions. Bank restructuring is taking place (see banking section in Chapter 3), but normalisation of relationships between creditors and debtors often involves lengthy negotiations. The banks may face higher than normal costs in identifying the true situation of firms. A number of problem debtors may become solvent at somewhat lower interest rates. In other cases, firms may have the capacity to sustain the burden implicit in currently high real interest rates, but they face uncertainty regarding their future sales and their future sources of finance. In addition, there may be willingness-to-pay problems, derived in part from moral hazard created by the bank loan restructuring programmes.

Both supply and demand side factors have inhibited growth in credit aggregates. The scope of financial intermediation has been reduced as the risks and costs involved have mounted. Banks have substantially tightened credit standards in the face of their recent experience. In part, this is a belated correction to upgrade previously inadequate controls, but the move also reflects the current cyclical situation. The combination of low levels of activity, reduced household revenues, and prevailing balance-sheet problems of households and firms has increased the difficulties in identifying good and bad credit risks and thus the risks attached to lending. Indeed, in many cases, the ability of potential creditors to pay has not been fully restored. There are also factors at play that dampen credit demand, most notably an increased aversion of borrowers towards high-gearing ratios and the pattern of the recovery until well into 1997: companies that

Figure 9. **MONETARY AGGREGATES**

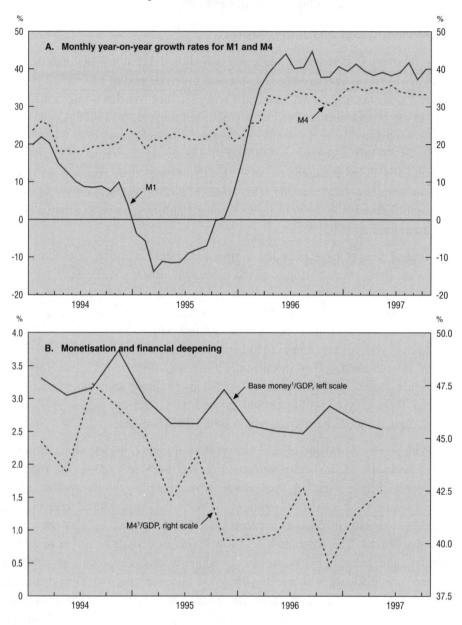

A. Monthly year-on-year growth rates for M1 and M4

M4

M1

B. Monetisation and financial deepening

Base money[1]/GDP, left scale

M4[1]/GDP, right scale

1.   End of quarter figures.
Source: OECD and Banco de México.

46

Table 9. **Bank lending and financial savings**

	Dec. 1993	Dec. 1994	Dec. 1995	Dec. 1996	Sep. 1997
	End-of-period stocks, billion pesos				
M4	587.7	729.1	880.1	1166.2	1401.9
Bank credit					
Total	450.5	639.9	810.4	909.7	934.1
To private sector	434.2	613.1	764.0	863.1	881.4
Excluding official asset purchases[1]	434.2	613.1	618.6	510.8	474.9
	Percentage year-on-year changes, in real terms				
M4	17.2	15.9	−20.6	3.8	12.8
Bank credit					
Total	9.7	32.7	−16.7	−12.1	−9.5
To private sector	15.9	31.9	−18.0	−11.5	−10.6
Excluding official asset purchases[1]	15.9	31.9	−33.6	−35.3	−22.7

1. Excludes assets that have been sold or transfered to trust funds in the context of debtor and bank support programmes.
Source: Banco de México.

have been doing well were mostly exporters with access to foreign exchange credits outside the peso-loan books of domestic banks.

The slowdown in credit growth also affected development banks, which in many cases have not made full use of available funds. These banks have traditionally played a role in reducing credit constraints on small and medium-size enterprises and on sectors that are not fully bankable. Their lending operations are conducted mainly by means of ''second-tier'' operations (*i.e.* through the intermediation of commercial banks). The banking crisis has limited the extent of these second-tier operations and some development banks moved back into direct lending operations on a limited scale.

Over time, with the unravelling of remaining problems between creditors and debtors, growth in financial savings is likely to be reflected in easier credit conditions. The improved liquidity position of banks should help sustain a recovery in bank lending as stronger output growth bolsters the creditworthiness of borrowers. Finally, credit market conditions are also set to improve as a result of lesser pressure on banks to provision for bad loans and improve their capitalisation.

Trends in interest rates, exchange rates and capital inflows

During 1996 and in the first three quarters of 1997, nominal and real interest rates eased in a climate of growing confidence, as the recovery gained momentum and inflation receded from its 1995 peak. The easing of interest rates reflected declining inflation expectations as the new policy framework established itself. Concomitant with the improving inflation performance over the last two years, there has been a convergence of private inflation expectations towards the official targets. Under the 1996 monetary programme, the inflation rate was cut roughly in half, and the further decline in inflation in 1997 brought the monthly inflation rate to below 1 per cent by mid-year. At the start of 1996, many private sector forecasts for inflation still exceeded 30 per cent, more that 10 percentage points above the official target. In mid-1997, private forecasts were centred only some 2 percentage points above the official 15 per cent inflation target. This suggests an improved credibility of the central bank's inflation target, which should facilitate guiding inflation further down in the coming period.

Successful pursuit of gradual disinflation has paid off in a progressive decline in the risk premium in interest rates as well; as a result, real interest rates declined from over 15 per cent in the second half of 1995 to about 8 per cent in mid-1997 (Figure 10). There was also a noticeable reduction in the spread between returns on the US money market and the ex-post dollar return of investments in the Mexican money market since 1995 (Figure 11, panel B). Confirmation of a sustained recovery in activity has reduced investors' uncertainty about Mexican markets. Furthermore, the exchange rate remained relatively stable and in fact stronger than assumed in the government's November 1996 macro projections underlying the budget. This favourable conjuncture of declining interest rates, a strong peso, and a recovery in the stock market took place in a context of ample international liquidity and an easing of US long-term interest rates that stimulated renewed capital inflows. Nevertheless, a large inflation premium still exists as evidenced by the spread between the return on indexed securities and the Cetes rate.

The volatility of both interest and exchange rates has been reduced since the height of the crisis in 1995.[23] The decline in market volatility, which can account in part for the reduction in real interest rates, is of particular importance given the persistent problem of over-indebtedness of firms and households. It has a positive effect by reducing uncertainty regarding the state of the banking system and the

Figure 10. **REAL RETURNS ON INDEXED BONDS AND MONEY MARKET INSTRUMENTS**

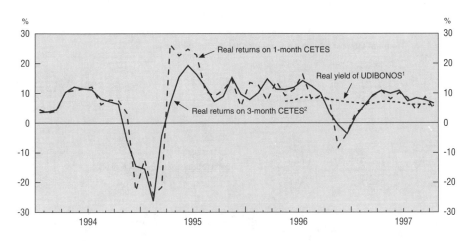

1.   UDIBONOS are bonds indexed to the Consumer Price Index.
2.   3-month CETES rate minus inflation in the current quarter.
Source: Banco de México.

potential fiscal cost of the bank rescue programme. More stable financial markets, in turn, can be conducive to debtors maintaining normal servicing of debts and financial intermediaries resuming lending activities.

Strong capital inflows are the response to several factors, and interest differentials only account for a part, but this part may increase as uncertainty diminishes. Large interest differentials *vis-à-vis* the US and a stable exchange rate have yielded high ex-post dollar returns. However, this does not seem to be the main factor driving capital inflows so far, as these large differentials may merely reflect the higher risk premium on peso-denominated assets. As discussed in Chapter I, short-term inflows into the money market were not predominant in 1995-96, with foreign direct investment flows (FDI) representing a large share of total foreign investment. The persistent strength of FDI – even during the crisis – may be a response to the low level of asset prices in Mexico, new investment opportunities brought about by NAFTA integration, and a heightened export competitiveness. In the first half of 1997, portfolio investment recovered swiftly, especially investments in long-term instruments, rising to twice the amount of

49

Figure 11. **DEVELOPMENTS IN FOREIGN EXCHANGE AND MONEY MARKETS**

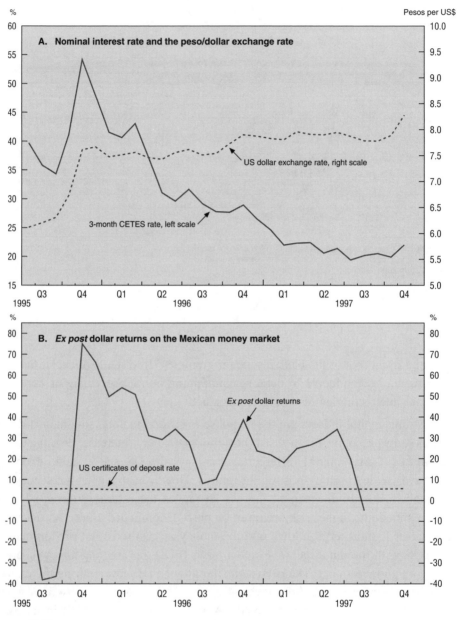

Source: OECD.

FDI; and several indicators suggest that they continued at a rapid pace in the third quarter of 1997 as the exchange rate firmed somewhat.

Challenges facing monetary policy

Progress has been made in the stabilisation of inflation expectations as the current framework for monetary policy was implemented. This is important to face the challenges that lie ahead in ensuring a smooth transition towards sustainable balanced growth. The main challenge may be how to sustain the pace of disinflation. Furthermore, monetary policy may have to contend with the pressures created by large and volatile portfolio capital inflows and potential risks of misalignment in the real exchange rate.

Generating a balanced recovery and minimising downside risks

The Mexican economy was in a process of adjustment to large structural changes when the 1994/95 crisis hit. The post-crisis adjustment may be, to some extent, part of a painful but necessary adjustment process which the crisis advanced. A reflection of this is the fact that the recovery has brought new job creation but not in the same sectors as those in which jobs were lost during the crisis. While the unemployment rate is back to 1994 levels, average earnings have declined. Cash flow and balance-sheet positions of firms producing for the domestic market remain weak.

The downside risks to the outlook are heightened by the exposure generated by the over-indebtedness of the private sector. Until cash-flow of firms and households recovers, the risk remains that such over-indebtedness will thwart medium-term prospects by putting pressure on the financial position of intermediaries, investment, and ultimately on the sustainability of the fiscal accounts. Two elements have contributed to reducing these downside risks: the first is that the recovery has continued at a strong pace, becoming more broadly based; the second is the greater stability in the financial environment, which has facilitated the decline in risk premia and in real interest rates; it is by this route in particular that monetary policy can continue to play an important role.

Sustaining the disinflation momentum

A key issue in setting policy is to determine the scope for additional disinflation and how fast to approach the long-term price stability objective of the

Central Bank (defined as inflation in the 0 to 3 per cent range). A swift move to lower inflation has been facilitated by maintenance of a strong fiscal position and greater stability in the nominal exchange rate. Data on prices of traded and non-traded goods suggest that a sustained decline in the relative price of non-traded goods has been a factor supporting rapid disinflation up to mid-1997, while the strength of the peso exchange rate has contained increases in prices of tradable goods. A strong sustained recovery of demand will probably limit somewhat the scope for rapid disinflation. On the other hand, the pass-through of exchange rate depreciation into domestic prices of tradable goods was apparently completed in the first semester of 1997 and dollar prices of tradable goods have recovered their pre-crisis levels. Thus, the influence of adjustment in tradable goods prices on inflation may diminish.

A clear commitment to price stability is an important element in the reduction of inflation uncertainties over a longer horizon. The Bank's 1995 policy document aimed at a return to single digit inflation within two years and gradual convergence to inflation of Mexico's main trading partners over the period up to the year 2000. The unexpected severity of the 1995 crisis forced a revision of the January 1995 programme. More recently, the government, in its medium-term programme (PRONAFIDE), has set out a less ambitious projection regarding the pace of disinflation in the period to 2000; inflation would be cut by at least 2.5 percentage points per year and by December 2000 would reach a rate of 7.5 per cent or less, this figure representing a ceiling rather than a target, in the context of macroeconomic policies that would, as central priorities, foster domestic saving and prevent excessive current account imbalances. It is important for the authorities to avoid creating a perception in the markets that greater priority will be given to maintaining a competitive exchange rate and sustainable current accounts rather than to the setting of ambitious annual inflation targets.

Meeting the challenge of capital inflows and exchange rate overshooting

A second challenge facing monetary policy is strong short-term capital inflows. Shifts in foreign portfolio investments have posed policy dilemmas in Mexico in the past. The current framework may however prove more appropriate to deal with these problems: under the current system of a floating exchange rate, the central bank can react to sustained short-term capital inflows by an easing of conditions in domestic money markets or by allowing the exchange rate to strengthen. The interest rate and the exchange rate responses have opposite effects on inflation, thus allowing the central bank to vary monetary conditions in order to seek a combination of interest rate easing and exchange rate appreciation (tightening) that is consistent with its inflation target. Nevertheless, surges in capital flows do pose a risk of high volatility and potential misalignment of the exchange rate. Of particular concern to authorities in the current context is the risk that surges in reversible capital flows drive up the real exchange rate and cause an unsustainable widening of the current account deficit. The Bank of Mexico announced, in its September policy report, that it will use an active interest rate policy in order to avoid exchange rate appreciation which it considers to be out of line with fundamentals; such interventions are conditioned on maintenance of a policy stance that is consistent with the overriding inflation objective. Difficulties may arise in policy implementation as meeting inflation and monetary targets would require that any stimulus provided by an easing of interest rates be compensated by an exchange rate appreciation. Under current conditions, it is difficult to judge to what extent changes in interest rates may under- or over-compensate for exchange rate movements. A second important factor is how banking sector problems may influence the transmission mechanism from changes in interest rates to demand and output. At present, changes in interest rates may have little impact on expansion of credit; their most important effect at this point may be to alter disposable income of over-indebted households and firms.

What is an appropriate level for the real exchange rate remains uncertain, not least because the different indicators provide a disparate picture of the current situation. While CPI-based measures of the real exchange rate show a strong upward trend, alternative measures of competitiveness based on unit labour costs show a very modest recovery from the 1995 trough. The slow recovery in prices of non-traded goods can in large part be explained by the weakness of domestic demand. The recovery in domestic prices and wages – relative to their international benchmarks – has taken place only gradually in line with the recovery in income flows and in domestic demand. Two additional sources of uncertainty concern the extent of structural change in the Mexican export sector and the size of sustainable capital inflows. In view of these uncertainties, allowance for flexibility in the adjustment of the real exchange rate should be seen as a positive feature of the current policy framework.

Fiscal Policy

Following the December 1994 peso crisis, fiscal policy was severely tightened to help narrow the gap between domestic saving and investment while providing for increased debt service payments on a dollar-linked public debt. The primary budget surplus widened to 4.6 per cent of GDP in 1995 (a 2.2 percentage point increase from 1994) while the economy went into a deep – though short-lived – recession. Towards the end of 1995, in view of the severity of the recession, and given improving investors' confidence, the emphasis of fiscal policy shifted from immediate post-crisis management to nurturing the recovery. When the budget for 1996 was prepared, the government's outstanding dollar-linked liabilities (*Tesobonos*) had for the most part been refinanced at longer-term maturity. The public sector net debt to GDP ratio remained relatively low – one of the lowest in the OECD area – despite an increase attributable to valuation effects of the foreign debt component. The current account deficit had been virtually eliminated (a 7 percentage point swing in relation to GDP), and inflation, although short of meeting the year-end target of 42 per cent, was declining. The budget for 1996 projected a zero deficit and a reduction in the primary surplus by an amount equivalent to 0.9 per cent of GDP.[24] The authorities became increasingly concerned about the potential fiscal costs of the measures that were being put in place to support banks and debtors, limiting the scope for additional fiscal policy relaxation. Resources were set aside in the 1995 and the 1996 fiscal exercises to cover part of these costs. The estimate of the total fiscal cost of the support package made in the budget for 1996 has since been revised upward (see Chapter III below).

Budgetary developments in 1996

In 1996, the financial accounts of the broad public sector[25] were close to balance, as budgeted. The 1996 outturn was achieved while making provisions to pay part of the fiscal cost of the support package to banks and debtors. Resources equivalent to 0.8 per cent of GDP were transferred from the Federal Government to FOBAPROA, the agency responsible for dealing with bank insolvencies, to amortise in advance part of its debt with the central bank.[26] Interest payments – including the transfers to FOBAPROA – amounted to 4.3 per cent of GDP. The primary surplus (financial balance less interest payments) turned out to be larger than projected, narrowing by 0.3 percentage point to 4.3 per cent of GDP (Table 10, Figure 12). This decline, in combination with output growth of 5 per cent, implies that fiscal policy in 1996 provided some demand stimulus, after the severe 1995 tightening.

Public sector revenue was budgeted to fall slightly in relation to GDP between 1995 and 1996 mostly reflecting the expected fall in public enterprise revenue. At the federal level, the decline in PEMEX contributions was expected to be partly offset by higher tax revenue (Table 11). However, as world oil prices continued to rise in 1996, PEMEX contributions to the federal budget exceeded projections by 1 percentage point of GDP, while tax revenue was lower than projected. As announced in the budget, tax incentives were granted to firms increasing investment and employment, and low-income households were exempted from income tax. In the event, the income tax component turned out to be broadly in line with projections; but VAT revenue and excise taxes did not pick up as expected.[27] Aggregate budgetary revenue of public enterprises fell in

Table 10. **Public sector financial accounts: budget and outturn**

Percentage of GDP

	Outturn 1994	Projected[1] 1995	Outturn 1995	Budget 1996	Outturn 1996	Budget 1997
Revenue	22.7	22.6	22.8	22.3	22.8	22.4
Expenditure	23.0	22.1	22.9	22.3	22.9	23.0
Financial balance[2]	**–0.1**	**0.4**	**0.0**	**0.0**	**0.0**	**–0.5**
Primary balance[3]	**2.2**	**3.9**	**4.6**	**3.7**	**4.3**	**3.4**
Public saving	**3.2**	**–**	**3.3**	**3.1**	**3.6**	**2.3**
Memorandum items:						
Interest payments, total	2.5	3.5	4.6	3.7	4.3	3.9
of which: Excluding provisions for support package cost	2.5	3.5	3.8	3.7	3.5	3.5
Provisions for support package cost[4]	–	–	0.8	–	0.8	0.4

1. Reinforced plan (March 1995).
2. "Economic balance" in the Mexican terminology.
3. Financial balance *less* net interest payments.
4. Deposit made to FOBAPROA to cover part of the cost of the support programmes for banks ans debtors (see section on banks in Part III below).
Source: Ministry of Finance.

Figure 12. **BUDGET INDICATORS**[1]
Per cent of GDP

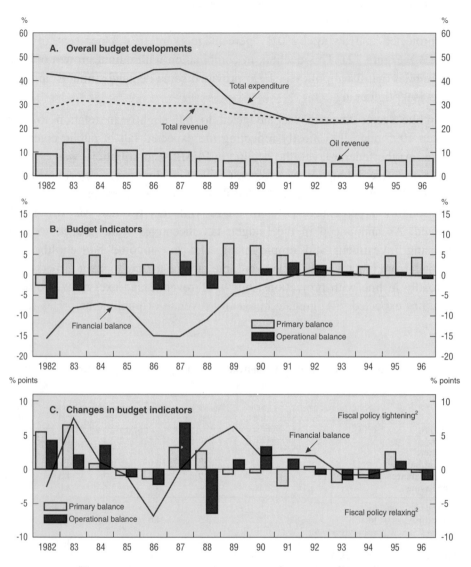

1. The public sector comprises federal government and public enterprises under budgetary control (such as PEMEX). Privatisation receipts and financial intermediation by development banks are not included; the financial balance is the "economic" balance according to the Mexican terminology; the primary balance is the financial balance less net interest payments while the operational balance is adjusted for inflation.
2. Tightening (relaxing) is defined as a widening (falling) surplus or narrowing (widening) deficit.
Source: Ministry of Finance, Banco de México.

Table 11. **Federal government budget**

Percentage of GDP

	1994	1995		1996		1977
	Outturn	Projected[1]	Outturn	Budget	Outturn	Budget
Revenue	**15.2**	**15.2**	**15.2**	**15.0**	**15.4**	**15.2**
Contribution of PEMEX	2.2	3.2	3.9	3.4	4.4	4.0
Other non-tax revenue	1.7	1.2	2.0	1.9	2.1	2.1
Tax revenue	11.3	10.8	9.3	9.8	8.9	9.1
of which:						
Income tax	5.1	4.1	4.0	3.8	3.8	3.5
VAT	2.7	3.8	2.8	3.3	2.8	2.8
Excise taxes	2.0	1.5	1.3	1.7	1.2	1.7
Import duties	0.9	0.9	0.6	0.6	0.6	0.5
Expenditure	**15.9**	..	**16.0**	**15.6**	**15.9**	**16.3**
Programmable	10.4	..	9.5	9.2	9.2	9.8
Current expenditure	8.3	..	7.8	..	7.5	8.7
Capital expenditure	2.4	..	1.9	..	1.9	1.7
Delayed payments	–0.4	–0.6	–0.2	–0.5	–0.2	–0.5
Non-programmable	5.5	..	6.6	6.4	6.7	6.5
Revenue sharing	2.9	..	2.7	3.0	2.8	2.8
Interest payments	2.0	..	3.8	2.9	3.7[2]	3.3[2]
Other[3]	0.5	..	0.1	0.4	0.2	0.4

1. Reinforced stabilisation plan (March 1995).
2. Interest payments indicated here for 1996 (outturn) and 1997 include provisions made on account of the support programmes for banks and debtors.
3. Includes accounts payable from previous fiscal period and net expenditure of the Federal Government on behalf of state-owned enterprises.

Source: Ministry of Finance.

relation to GDP, in line with projections (Table 12). The social security institutions IMSS and ISSSTE in particular continued to record significant reductions in real revenue as a result of the decline in real average wages on which contributions are levied.

Public expenditure rose by 3.3 per cent in real terms in 1996. Interest payments (including resources set aside to cover the fiscal cost of the bank support scheme) fell in real terms, reflecting lower funding costs on foreign debt and the decline in domestic interest rates. On the other hand, non-interest spending rose by 4.8 per cent in real terms, but relative to GDP it was still well below its level in 1994, reflecting the severity of the 1995 cuts. As projected in the budget, the increase in public spending was concentrated on economic infrastructure and social programmes. The Federal Government increased resources spent

Table 12. **Public enterprises under budgetary control: financial accounts**[1]

Percentage of GDP

	1994	1995		1996		1977
	Outturn	Projected[2]	Outturn	Budget	Outturn	Budget
Revenue	**8.8**	..	**8.9**	**8.3**	**8.6**	**8.6**
PEMEX	2.2	2.6	2.7	2.9	2.9	3.0
Other public enterprises	5.3	4.7	4.8	4.4	4.4	4.2
Transfers received	1.3	..	1.4	1.0	1.2	1.4
Expenditure	**8.4**	..	**8.3**	**7.8**	**8.2**	**8.0**
Current expenditure	6.2	..	5.9	5.4	5.6	5.7
Capital expenditure	1.8	..	1.6	1.7	2.0	1.7
Interest payments	0.4	..	0.8	0.7	0.6	0.6

1. State-owned enterprises under budgetary control, excluding public financial intermediaries (development banks and development trust funds).
2. Reinforced stabilisation plan (March 1995).
Source: Ministry of Finance.

directly on social development as well as transfers to the states in the context of increasing decentralisation.

The increase in non-interest expenditure of the broad public sector is entirely attributable to the rise in capital expenditure (up by about 10 per cent in real terms), which in relation to GDP was restored to its 1994 level.[28] Programmes were put in place to enhance PEMEX productive capacity, develop the national electricity company's (CFE) distribution system and build new roads. On the other hand, the public sector wage bill (accounting for 41 per cent of budget expenditure), expanded by less than 1 per cent in real terms, despite significant increases in the health and education sectors. A number of public enterprises were privatised in 1996, and the process was engaged for others.[29]

The 1997 Budget

The Budget for 1997, released in November 1996, aimed at consolidating the ongoing recovery, but again fiscal policy was cautious, safeguarding strong public sector financial balances. A small financial deficit of the public sector – equivalent to 0.5 per cent of GDP – was budgeted, including the coverage of the expected cost of the pension and health insurance reform (estimated at about 0.7 per cent of GDP for the second half of 1997) and making provisions to pay part of the cost of support programmes for banks and debtors (0.4 per cent of GDP). The primary surplus was projected to fall to 3.4 per cent of GDP,[30] while interest payments *stricto sensu* (excluding provisions for the support package) were projected to increase by 0.3 percentage point of GDP. On the basis of the Ministry of Finance's most recent estimates, the budget outturn is likely to be close to projections, and the primary surplus is expected to reach 3.7 per cent of GDP, down 0.6 percentage point from the 1996 outturn. At the same time, real GDP is estimated to have grown by close to 7 per cent in 1997.

Going beyond the confines of the budget numbers, the emphasis of fiscal policy in 1997 has been on intensifying the fight against tax evasion and avoidance, and on simplifying tax and customs administration.[31] With the recovery more mature, tax incentives to job creation and investment introduced in 1996 have been scaled down. Instead, priorities are shifting to developing basic infrastructure in communications and transport, water, oil and electricity sectors. Investment financed by budget allocation are being complemented by a new financing mechanism: the government contracts out projects to private enterprises for building and then transferring the projects back to the public sector for operation upon completion; payment from budget resources takes place after completion only.[32] Current outlays not related to social programmes are being given low priority.

Financial accounts for the broad public sector in the first nine months of 1997 show a stronger fiscal position than envisaged in the initial budget: a budget surplus of 0.6 per cent of GDP was achieved in January-September, although, given usual seasonal patterns of government transactions, and the increased expenditure entailed by the social security reform since July 1997, the outturn is likely to be different for the year as a whole. Interest payments on the public debt were significantly lower than a year earlier, while non-interest expenditure expanded briskly (12.9 per cent in real terms). The public sector wage bill recorded a substantial increase in real terms; fixed investment and revenue sharing transfers continued to grow rapidly. A significant difference from the outturn in 1996 is the recovery of non-oil revenue that occurred in the first nine months of 1997. The federal government tax revenue was up 9.5 per cent in real terms from a year earlier, as a result of the upturn of economic activity and (perhaps) of more effective tax collection as well.

Debt management

After the peso crisis, the most urgent task for public debt management was to refinance and extend the maturity of short-term dollar linked securities (*Tesobonos*). This was achieved by the end of 1995, mainly through longer-term borrowing from the US government and the IMF financial assistance package. In addition, during 1995, public sector entities (federal government, development banks and PEMEX essentially) were able to issue bonds on international capital markets for increasing amounts and under rapidly improving borrowing conditions. As a result, the net debt of the public sector including federal government, public enterprises and development banks rose to 38.9 per cent of GDP in December 1995, a 1.3 percentage point increase above the level a year earlier, attributable to valuation effects.[33] By then, the external component accounted for nearly all of the public net debt.

With their most immediate objective accomplished by January 1996, the Mexican authorities focused on lowering the funding costs and lengthening the average maturity of the public debt. Accelerated repayment of the US government loan, first in August 1996 for US$7 billion (about two-thirds of the US credit outstanding) and again in January 1997 for the remaining US$3.5 billion, served this purpose. Between August 1996 and April 1997, Mexico also made early payments on its obligations to the IMF (for an amount equivalent to US$3.7 billion). Foreign investors' rapidly improving confidence permitted refinancing of the financial assistance package ahead of schedule on increasingly favourable borrowing conditions. Developments in 1997 are further evidence of this progress. In August, for instance, the Federal government prepaid the outstanding floating rate notes due in 2001 (a total amount of US$6 billion) which had themselves been issued a year earlier for the repayment on the US loan mentioned above.[34] The relatively stable exchange rate and the strengthening of GDP in 1996 and 1997 have allowed a gradual lowering of the net public external debt in relation to GDP – down 6 percentage points of GDP over the twelve months to December 1996, and by 4 percentage points in the first nine months of 1997.

The same strategy of lengthening the maturity was applied to the domestic debt, which stood at 6.2 per cent of GDP in 1995 and 1996 (for the net debt). By issuing on an increasing scale *Bondes* (1-2 year treasury bills) and *Udibonos* (3-5 year indexed bonds), the government managed to lengthen the average maturity of the domestic debt from 283 days at end 1995 to 342 days in

September 1997.[35] The small proportion of the domestic debt in the total appears to be justified currently by the very large differences in funding costs on the domestic relative to foreign markets. In the longer run, however, as borrowing conditions converge, the authorities may allow some shift of the debt towards a build-up of the domestic component. Such a move would also facilitate the operations of the privatised pension funds (see Chapter III below).

A medium-term policy framework: PRONAFIDE 1997-2000

In June 1997, the government presented a medium-term macro-economic scenario, the National Programme for Financing Development, 1997-2000 (PRONAFIDE), setting the policy framework for the remaining period of the current administration. The programme, which elaborates on the government's broad strategy presented in the "National Development Plan, 1995-2000", provides an explicit statement of the principles that will guide policy making over the 3-4 years ahead so as to maintain a stable macroeconomic environment. In the past, typically, the public in Mexico has had to wait till the last months of the year to find out what policies for the coming year would be. The social pact signed in September/October, the budget presented to Parliament in November and the monetary programme announced at the turn of the year have between them served that purpose, but the time horizon was limited to a single year. There was clearly a need for a medium-term policy framework providing information and explanations about where the economy was heading and the concomitant policy stance. As argued in the OECD *Economic Surveys* of 1995 and 1996, this could serve to stabilise private sector expectations, thereby facilitating effective planning (investment, borrowing decisions...) and contribute to reducing the risk premium in interest rates. The PRONAFIDE is intended to fill this role.

Main elements of the programme

The PRONAFIDE establishes a quantitative baseline scenario for main macroeconomic variables (growth of aggregate output and demand components, inflation, the current balance), focusing on the links between saving and investment, and between physical investment and medium-term growth of (potential) output. It stresses the importance of domestic saving to finance investment, with foreign saving playing a complementary – but limited – role, so as to reduce the economy's vulnerability to changes in foreign investors' sentiment. The baseline scenario envisages a gradual return to a growth rate of 5.6 per cent at the end of the period, led by exports and investment, while consumption picks up slowly (Table 13). This rate of growth is viewed by the government as necessary to absorb the expected increase in the labour force. Inflation is kept on a declining path, falling to 7.5 per cent by 2000, the numbers retained in the exercise representing a ceiling rather than a target. More generally, the macroeconomic variables in the PRONAFIDE are presented not as forecasts but rather as trend evolutions that serve as a benchmark, while developments from one year to another could fluctuate around the baseline.[36] The scenario implicitly suggests that the authorities set a ceiling on the current account deficit (a little above 3 per cent of GDP) which is seen as sustainable because it would be entirely financed by long-term capital inflows (foreign direct investment) – a benchmark from which the external account should not be allowed to diverge significantly.

Table 13. **The government's medium-term scenario**

	1997	1998	1999	2000
Demand and output (volume)[1]				
Total consumption	2.9	3.9	4.0	4.7
of which: Private	3.2	4.0	4.2	5.0
Total investment	14.5	10.6	10.4	10.7
of which: Private	21.3	16.4	13.4	12.7
Exports of goods and services	12.6	10.6	10.0	10.0
Imports of goods and services	15.7	12.6	11.0	11.8
GDP	**4.5**	**4.8**	**5.2**	**5.6**
Inflation (December to December)[1]	**15.0**	**12.5**	**10.0**	**7.5**
Aggregate saving[2]				
Gross domestic saving	20.6	21.0	21.6	22.2
Public	4.3	3.9	4.4	4.5
Private	16.3	17.1	17.3	17.7
Foreign saving	1.6	2.2	2.6	3.2
Current account balance (US$ billion)	**–6.0**	**–9.1**	**–11.6**	**–15.3**
Public sector financial balance[2]	**–0.5**	**–1.3**	**–0.8**	**–0.3**

1. Percentage change.
2. Percentage of GDP.
Source: Federal Government, *National Programme for Financing Development, 1995-2000* (PRONAFIDE).

Evaluation

The PRONAFIDE document stresses the importance of policies that enhance saving: high domestic saving allows high investment, which is indispensable to facilitate rapid growth; at the same time it is key to avoid excessive reliance on foreign saving and thus an unsustainable deterioration in the current balance. Given the nature of past crises, it seems appropriate that the medium-term projections focus on the saving-investment balance and the current balance constraint. But this should not be (mis-) interpreted as a causal analysis of the mechanism of sustained growth. Ultimately it is the growth of labour efficiency that facilitates sustainable output growth per capita. By raising the productivity of capital, it provides strong investment incentives; where the high marginal productivity of capital is allowed to translate into high real returns on private saving, the latter is likely to increase. The causal chain sketched above suggests that the policies trying to stimulate growth must first of all strengthen measures to raise labour efficiency, rather than focus solely on the promotion of investment and saving.

Indeed, the PRONAFIDE recognises that growth depends on technological progress and improving labour productivity and stresses the importance of investing in education, training, adequate nutrition and health care, as well as developing infrastructure and modernising the financial system. Thus, by linking macroeconomic performance to structural reform, the programme offers a rather comprehensive policy framework. Likewise, recent policy initiatives conducive to higher private saving are recalled: the pension reform implemented in mid-1997, tax measures already taken (the 1995 VAT rate increase), modernisation of the financial sector – an appropriate recognition of the importance of structural measures. At the same time the programme recognises that strong public finances will be needed, first to maintain significant public saving, until the private component has strengthened; second to cover contingent liabilities related to the social security reform and bank and debtor support schemes. Although uncertainties are great in this domain, an attempt has been made to quantify the potential fiscal costs of the various measures, and estimates of the pressure on public finances is provided for each year to 2000.

While recognising that the PRONAFIDE is a valuable orientation concerning medium-term policies, a number of issues merits examination:

- The projections appear cautious in several respects, which may help to enhance the credibility of the exercise. For instance the projected output growth is just sufficient to absorb labour force growth in the formal segment of the labour market, while reducing very gradually the current degree of labour market slack. GDP growth in 1997 is very likely to be much stronger than shown in the scenario, and if the current fiscal and monetary policy stances are maintained, the same could be true for 1998. Also, given the current stance of policies and declared central bank objectives, the inflation rate projected for the end of 1998 (and 2000) appears to be on the high side.[37]
- Domestic saving may turn out to be lower than projected. The main risk relates to the behaviour of households. Given the fall in real wages in the wake of the 1994/95 peso crisis, it is likely that the future increase in real income will be used to restore previous real consumption levels rather than be saved. If the increase in the domestic saving ratio recorded in 1995 and 1996 is mainly due to a redistribution of income from low- to high-income households, its sustainability is indeed questionable.[38]
- The current account deficit projections appear to be on the low side; they imply a significant reduction in income elasticities of imports. While the structural changes undergone over recent years may justify this assumption, it is too soon to tell. The flexible exchange rate regime, however, provides an automatic adjustment mechanism. The assumed rapid increase in the stock of foreign direct investment is also likely to induce large factor service payments, which will put pressure on the current account.
- Regarding domestic saving, it is unclear to what extent the pension reform (reviewed in Chapter III) will affect the household saving ratio over the horizon of the PRONAFIDE, though it is hoped that it will raise private saving in the long run. On the other hand, securing access of small savers to competitive and undistorted capital markets may raise household saving by providing access to higher real returns.[39] In this context increased competition in the banking sector should lead to the development of a network to collect small deposits, creating favourable conditions for higher private saving, and their more efficient use.[40]

– Only public saving can be directly influenced by government action. The announced tax measures which aim at increasing the tax base and improving tax collection are appropriate from a public finance point of view, as they might strengthen non-oil revenue.

Several of the issues that are raised in the PRONAFIDE will remain important over the medium-term, going beyond the year 2000. The foremost of these is the sustainability of the current account deficit, which – among other factors – depends importantly on the way it is financed. It is unclear whether and how the government can influence the composition of net capital inflows. Second, measures to improve tax collection, as envisaged in the PRONAFIDE, can loosen some of the constraints under which fiscal policy is operating. Because of the narrowness of tax base, tax revenue is very small in proportion to GDP, and so is government expenditure in the face of large and urgent needs for developing human capital and physical infrastructure. In this context, it is worth noting that a substantial part of government revenue is based on income from oil exploitation, which in economic terms (as opposed to national accounting terms) represents ''destocking'' (*i.e.* a reduction in non-renewable resources). As government oil revenues exceed public sector saving, it can thus be argued that the latter is actually negative in economic terms, which can justify a substantial increase in government saving, *e.g.* by significant increases in taxes. Mexico's very low tax/GDP ratio, both absolute and in relation to the country's per capita income, would support such a proposition (see Figure 13 in Chapter III). The recognised backlog in infrastructure (including social development infrastructure such as sewage systems, drinking water, etc.) would provide profitable investment outlets for the implied increase in public saving.

These considerations lead on to some key questions not addressed in the PRONAFIDE: the first relates to the policy dilemma that large and volatile capital inflows may create in the future (as discussed in the section above).[41] The second concerns the longer-term growth rate of the Mexican economy. The scenario is designed as a benchmark to facilitate the monitoring of economic developments in the remaining years of the current administration. Setting such a benchmark for the conduct of policy is welcome since it can orient and stabilise expectations of market participants. With time it will become increasingly important to find ways to provide information about key aspects of policy orientation beyond the year 2000 – perhaps by rolling-over the medium-term scenario to help reduce uncertainties which are likely to emerge towards the end of the Presidential *"sexenio"*. The pertinent question that needs to be addressed is how Mexico can achieve strong sustainable growth – close to 6 per cent annual growth, which in the government's view is required to reduce labour market slack in the urban informal sector as well as rural under-employment. It is in this context that the following chapter reviews recent progress in implementing structural reform.

III. Implementing structural reform: a review of progress

Since the first Peso crisis in 1982 and the subsequent reorientation of its development strategy, Mexico has implemented wide-ranging structural reforms. The liberalisation and deregulation of the economy at first concentrated on product markets and on the financial system, while the labour market was left relatively untouched. The current administration, in its Development Plan for 1995-2000, has recognised the need to examine the institutional framework and policies pertaining to labour markets and social security to identify areas where reforms may be needed to improve conditions for higher sustainable output and employment growth. As evidenced in last year's OECD *Economic Survey* on Mexico, the structure and performance of the Mexican labour market differ significantly from those of most other OECD countries. Problems in Mexico do not manifest themselves in high open unemployment – with no unemployment insurance, most people have to engage in some kind of activity – but rather in the form of a dual labour market with a large proportion of the labour force occupied in low productivity jobs in the urban informal sector and in subsistence agriculture in rural areas – characteristic of countries lagging in development.

The December 1996 Survey stressed general directions for reform in the context of the OECD's *Jobs Study* (Table 14). Enhancing human capital, nurturing an entrepreneurial climate and developing infrastructure are conducive to a sustainable increase in living standards, which is the foremost challenge facing Mexico. Initiatives aimed at deregulating the labour market and making the tax and transfer system more effective can contribute to lowering barriers that currently keep many activities "informal". This chapter reviews recent measures related to labour markets and the social security reform. It then reports on the process of privatisation and regulatory reforms that is underway and administra-

Table 14. **Implementing the OECD jobs strategy – an overview**

Jobs strategy proposals[1]	Action taken	OECD assessment/recommendations
1. Enhance human capital		
• Introduce standardised competency and skill tests (certification)	– Under study	– Implement as early as possible
• Strengthen vocational/technical education (short cycle)	– Coverage has been extended	
• Continue targeted programmes to the poorest	– Reinforced action in 1996, more clearly defined in 1997	
• Provide basic health package	– Introduced in 1996, expanded in 1997	– Consider contracting-out arrangements to various public or private providers, when possible
2. Reform the tax and transfer system		
• Increase effectiveness of taxation	– Tax administration is being modernised	
• Public housing scheme (INFONAVIT)	– Administrative reform under way	– Proceed in line with proposals; establish pertinent regulations
• Implement the new pension system	– Regulations established, AFORES operating as of July 1997	
3. Improve infrastructure and foster small enterprise dynamism		
• Develop infrastructure	– Increased public investment and private participation	– A large backlog persists but cannot be eliminated immediately
• Further simplify bureaucratic requirements for SMEs and micro-enterprises	– Continued in 1997	
4. Increase the flexibility of employment regulation		
• Review employment protection provisions	– No action	– Consider options as window of opportunity is created
• Broaden scope for short-term contracts	– No action	
• Allow probationary periods	– No action	
5. Modernise the collective bargaining framework	– No action	

1. Proposals are discussed in detail in OECD (1996), Chapter III and Box 1.
Source: OECD.

tive reforms aimed at raising public sector efficiency. The final section provides an update on developments in the banking sector.[42]

Labour markets and related issues

Following the strategy outlined in the government's Development Plan 1995-2000 and consistent with the recommendations of the 1996 *Economic Survey,* additional resources were allocated to education and training in 1996-97 (although the increase served largely to reverse cuts undertaken in 1995). In basic as well as vocational/technical education, where acute needs have been identified, new teachers were hired and trained, and new buildings and equipment were put in operation. Special attention was given to education in remote areas and for marginal groups, through reinforced targeting of programmes and use of tele-education, in order to help create more equal opportunities across regions and income levels.[43] Recent efforts have yielded positive results: educational achievements, which had already marked some progress in 1995-96, further improved in 1996-97, in terms of increased basic education coverage and reduced drop-out and repetition rates (Federal government, 1997). Support to basic education has been linked to basic health and nutrition support. The pertinent poverty alleviation programme (PROGRESA) was introduced in August 1997 to provide a formal structure to the integrated approach gradually being put in place over the past few years. It includes money payments targeted to families in extreme poverty, conditional on school attendance by children and regular visits to health clinics. By the end of 1997, 400 000 families from 10 states are expected to have received support through PROGRESA.

The main purpose of active labour market programmes (ALMP) – training, direct job creation in the public sector and employment subsidies – is to facilitate workers' insertion into a productive activity. In the absence of any unemployment benefit system, some of the components of ALMP are the only kind of income support available in Mexico, with public placement services mainly having an information role. Recognising the need to enhance the ability of labour to adapt to the competitive environment, the Mexican authorities developed two main training schemes in the late 1980s: the first one to provide short-term grants and training to the unemployed (PROBECAT); the second one for training support in small and medium size enterprises (CIMO). The scale of these pro-

Table 15. **Active labour market policies**[1]

In thousands

	1994	1995	1996	January-September	
				1996	1997
Public employment services					
Job applications	489	533	455	381	351
Vacancies	357	326	343	274	328
People placed in a job	129	124	127	100	112
Training support for SMEs (CIMO)[2]					
Workers supported	150	368	549	309	306
Enterprises supported	46	105	175	95	110
Enterprises receiving other services	16	19	17	12[3]	13[3]
Training scholarships (PROBECAT)					
Scholarships for the unemployed	199	410	544	352	419
Trainee courses	8	23	27	18	21

1. For details on ALMP, see OECD (1996), *Economic Survey of Mexico*.
2. Training assistance programme for micro, small and medium-sized enterprises.
3. January-August.
Source: Ministry of Labour and Social Security (STPS).

grammes has increased significantly since 1993.[44] In the aftermath of the 1994/95 peso crisis, the government used them to some degree to provide an emergency safety net to those who had lost their jobs, thus altering and – given experience elsewhere in the OECD area – possibly compromising the original purpose they were to serve. Income support following the peso crisis also took the form of emergency job creation programmes set up specifically for that purpose: the Temporary Employment Programme (TEP) and the Rural Road Maintenance Programme were introduced in 1995, offering jobs to improve infrastructure in rural areas where poverty was the most acute. In 1996, the two emergency programmes together provided about 1 million temporary jobs.

Despite recent increases, the share of GDP Mexico spends on ALMP measures remains small compared with other OECD countries. In 1997, because the immediate post-crisis hardship had subsided, emergency measures were scaled down. The size of training programmes remained broadly in line with that of a year earlier, but they can now be more focused on their original purpose, which is important. The effectiveness of these programmes in promoting skill formation and workforce adaptability depends on the application of rigorous selection mechanisms. The special emergency measures put in place in 1995-1996 were not continued as such in 1997, but the TEP was maintained as an instrument for poverty alleviation, targeted at remote areas where job opportunities are scarce independently of cyclical conditions.

Although the labour market has demonstrated its flexibility in coping with severe shocks in the past, rapid changes in the economy create both needs and opportunities for modernising the institutional structure of the labour market. The signing in August 1996 of an agreement between social partners defining principles of a ''New Labour Culture'' can provide a basis for reviewing labour market practices, institutional arrangements and related regulations. In 1997, about a year later, against a background of improved economic conditions, the new political situation in Congress and recent changes in union leadership open a window of opportunity for such a review. The authorities should seize the opportunity to examine institutional arrangements. In a number of cases, it would be appropriate to bring formal regulations closer to actual practices; measures like broadening the scope of temporary contracts (recognised in the law for specific tasks) and allowing probationary periods for long-term contracts, as well as some easing of job protection provisions for permanent workers, could facilitate employment creation in the formal sector.[45]

The new pension system

The reform of the social security system (IMSS) which went into effect in mid-1997 seeks to address financial and efficiency concerns.[46] Measures taken, concerning both pensions and health insurance, are likely to affect the labour market and job creation. In particular, they are expected over time to induce a shift of employment from the informal to the formal sector by reducing payroll taxes (as a result of the financing reform of the health fund) and increasing the attractiveness of the pension system, in particular because pension rights for workers affiliated to IMSS become fully portable. The health component of the IMSS reform will be analysed in the following chapter, while recent developments in the pension segment are reviewed here.[47]

The pension reform, which became effective on 1 July 1997, has transformed the previous pay-as-you-go system (PAYG) into a fully-funded capitalisation system. The new system operates with individual pension accounts managed by private fund administrators (AFOREs). In addition to mandatory contributions, workers can make voluntary deposits on their accounts, and the government pays in a fixed contribution. Employers' contributions to the housing fund (INFONAVIT) are registered in these individual accounts. The main features of the regulations and the functioning of individual accounts are described in Box 2. Pensions accumulated by a worker affiliated to IMSS are fully portable and, on retirement, the worker will buy an annuity with the accumulated contributions.[48] In addition to the contribution size and the period over which pensions are paid, a key determinant of the pension level will be the rate of return earned on the individual account (after deduction of management fees). The level of pensions in some cases may be less favourable under the new regime than under the defined benefit system that operated prior to the reform, but the latter was not viable. Workers already contributing under the old system can choose upon retirement under which system they will receive benefits. There is a government guaranteed minimum pension equivalent to the minimum wage. If accumulated rights result in a pension lower than its level, the government will finance the necessary amount to provide the minimum guaranteed pension, funded out of general tax revenue.

The cost of the transition from the old PAYG system to the new scheme is officially estimated at 0.7 to 1 per cent of GDP annually over the next 20 years or so, gradually falling below $1/2$ per cent over the longer run.[49] This cost will be paid out of the general government budget. By paying the transition cost, the government is reducing an implicit government debt. The new pension system will also have implications for financial markets. The move to a privately run fully funded system for old-age pensions will create a demand for financial instruments that is likely to become a major factor shaping the future of the Mexican financial system. The new system will generate a flow of saving directed into the AFOREs accounts. The investment rules of the pension funds will play an important role in orienting this new demand for financial instruments. The pension fund administrators may find that initially there is not an abundant supply of eligible securities. The domestic public sector debt is small and unlikely to grow given low fiscal deficits. Furthermore, the supply of high quality private paper remains limited, as the 1995 financial crisis reduced the creditworthiness of major non-financial issuers on domestic capital markets. With time, the authorities intend to expand the range of investment options and allow equity

Box 2. **Main features of the individual pension accounts**

The individual accounts are managed by private administrators of pension funds (AFOREs), which invest the retirement savings in financial markets through specialised mutual funds (SIEFOREs), under the regulation and the supervision of the National Commission for the Retirement Saving System (CONSAR). Each account has three components, of which the first two are funded through compulsory contributions:

i) The retirement sub-account whose funds will cover severance payments and pension benefits in old age, financed by a tripartite contribution. The Federal government's social contribution is deposited in that segment, as well as contributions until now paid into the SAR account (2 per cent of the worker's salary; items 3, 4 and 5 in Table 16).

ii) The housing promotion sub-account receives the contribution to INFONAVIT (previously deposited in the SAR accounts); the funds, registered by the AFOREs, continue to be managed by INFONAVIT (item 6).

iii) A voluntary contribution sub-account (item 7).

A central register, which receives the funds from the collecting banks, will record the sums for each worker and transfer them to the AFORE selected by the worker for investment and management of the account.

By mid-1997, the CONSAR had authorised 17 AFOREs, most of them owned by banks and financial groups, including some with US partners. The approved AFOREs began registering workers as of February 1997 and have been receiving funds since September.

The CONSAR has established regulations aimed at ensuring competition between AFOREs, and it has defined an investment regime for mutual funds with the objective to provide workers with an adequate rate of return at acceptable risk. In the first year of operation, each AFORE is authorised to manage only one fund, investing at least 65 per cent in government securities, the rest in paper with public credit rating; with time they will manage several funds, with more diversified portfolios.

Each worker is allowed to change his AFORE once a year at no cost, and within the chosen AFORE, he will be able after the first year to choose among various investment funds. The contributions of workers who do not choose an AFORE are deposited in a "concentrating" account at the central bank under the IMSS' name. If no AFORE is selected, after four years the accounts will be transferred to one chosen by the regulatory agency.

No single AFORE can receive more than 17 per cent of aggregate retirement savings; the limit increases to 20 per cent after four years.

(continued on next page)

(continued)

Table 16. **The pension system after the IMSS reform**

Panel A. Contributions to pension scheme and disability insurance after the IMSS reform

	Premium (per cent of wage)	Cap (times the minimum wage)	Financing
1. Disability and life insurance	2.5	15-25[1]	Tripartite[2]
2. Retirees' medical care	1.5	15-25[1]	Tripartite[2]
3. Retirement and old-age severance	4.5	15-25[1]	Tripartite[2]
4. Government's contribution	365 pesos[3]	–	Government
5. Retirement saving (SAR)	2.0	15-25[1]	Employer
6. INFONAVIT	5.0	10	Employer
7. Voluntary contributions	–	–	Employee or employer

Panel B. Right to benefits

	Old scheme	New scheme
Minimum pension guaranteed by state	After 10 years of contributions	After 24 years of contributions
Workers who stop contributing before age 60/65	No right to pension	Get back amount accumulated on account
Workers who have been contributing to the former pension system	Choice of benefit formula on retirement	

Panel C. Pension levels[4] (times the minimum wage)

	Old scheme		New scheme	
	Inflation		Real interest rate	
	10 per cent	20 per cent	2.5 per cent	5 per cent
When contribution was based on:				
2 minimum wages	1.4	1.2	1.0	1.5
6 minimum wages	4.0	3.0	2.0	5.0

1. Rising from 15 minimum wages in 1997 to 25 minimum wages in 2007.
2. Employer 70 per cent, worker 25 per cent and government 5 per cent of total.
3. At 1997 constant prices, amount equivalent to 5.5 per cent of the minimum wage in the Federal district, indexed to this minimum wage.
4. Under the assumption that the individual receives a pension during 21 years after contributing to the scheme for 30 years.
Source: OECD Secretariat on the basis of information provided by national authorities.

investments. The demand created by the pension funds is likely to stimulate development of a more active and a deeper securities market.

Removing barriers to private initiative

The current phase of state retrenchment from the economy that started in 1995 under the new administration differs in two main respects from the previous phase:

i) Whereas the first round of state retrenchment – mostly completed by 1992 – consisted mainly of actual sales of public assets, the process now consists of opening sectors of activity dominated by state owner-ship (such as rail transportation, satellite telecommunications, and energy) to private initiative and competition largely through auctioning of concessions. The revenue that can be expected from the current operations is not as large as in the previous phase, but the potential impact on the economy can nevertheless be important because of the efficiency gains in the sectors involved and repercussions on other sectors of activity.

ii) The operations are no longer conducted under the sole authority of the Ministry of Finance, as was the case previously, but involve the various Ministries concerned. An inter-sectoral Commission for divestiture (*Comisión Intersecretarial de Desincorporación*) was created in 1995 to co-ordinate and supervise divestiture processes and within which regulatory issues may be examined. It brings together on a permanent basis five government authorities (the Federal Competition Commission, the Ministry of Finance, the Ministry of Trade and Industry, the Ministry of Labour and the Comptroller general), with other Ministries joining in accordance with the area being examined (transport and communications, energy, agriculture, etc.).

The Commission has a mandate to make recommendations to introduce a com-petitive environment prior to privatisation or granting concessions. Consequently, regulations governing the various areas being opened to private initiative have been issued. The constitution was amended to redefine – and in the process narrow – the scope of strategic sectors that remain exclusively reserved for State participation. Oil extraction and eight basic petrochemicals still belong to that core area, while secondary petrochemicals were opened to private participation.

Several steps were taken in the last year or so to advance further in the concession and privatisation of key sectors of activity, including network infrastructure industries (such as railroads, natural gas and electricity).[50] In railroad transportation services, the auctioning of three main railroad sections is underway. For the Northeast line, one of the country's busiest, the concession was sold to a Mexican-US consortium at the beginning of 1997. The Pacific-North section was sold in August 1997, including a concession to operate the line during 50 years. The last of the three big railroad lines, Southwest, is being auctioned before the end of 1997; this operation also includes a sale of stocks and a concession. If the project materialises, by end 1997, all railroad services will have been divested. Auctioning of stocks with concessions was facilitated by the fact that part of the proceeds were set aside to create a reserve fund to secure accrued pension rights of the national railroad workers.

In the telecommunications sector, competition in long distance service began in January 1997 in major cities, after the relevant regulations had become operational. Private firms who were granted the licenses committed themselves to making substantial investments in the sector (for a total amount of US$4.8 billion by the year 2004). Privatisation of the satellite fixed services takes two forms: first, granting concessions to use frequency bands in the radio-wave spectrum; for these, open auctions are programmed through the year 1997. Second, selling-off three existing satellites and various orbital slots and control centres. As a first step, a satellite company that manages all satellite services was created. Then, in the first half of 1997, regulations were established. The privatisation of the company started in the third quarter of the year: a majority stake (75 per cent) was sold in October and the remaining shares will be placed on the stock market in two or three years.

Regarding other network infrastructure industries, such as natural gas and electricity, revisions to the legal framework governing private investment and relevant regulations were finalised in March 1997. To promote participation of private entrepreneurs (domestic and foreign) in the distribution of *natural gas*, 16 geographic zones were defined, and auctioning of concessions pertaining to these zones has started. In some zones, where a substantial infrastructure (pipelines) is already in place, it is leased to the purchaser of the concession. In all regions, the permit holder is required to construct new pipeline networks and operate them.[51] By mid-1997, two permits had been awarded, several other public auctions being planned in the second half of the year. In the *electricity sector*, private participation is allowed in power generation: several power plant construction projects have already been authorised, contracts being awarded to Mexican and foreign investors. The electricity generated in private plants is to be sold to the national electricity company (CFE) which retains its monopoly on transmission, transformation and distribution of electricity.[52] The combination of private participation in power generation and increased public investment to develop the transmission and distribution capacity – as achieved in 1996 and budgeted in 1997 – can help meet rapidly rising demand from domestic users (firms and households), and should allow an appropriate diversification of energy supply. Conditions are thus created for splitting electricity generation completely from the transmission and distribution business. Such separation has been introduced in a number of countries as a means to encourage greater competition and consequent efficiency gains in the generating sector.

In the petrochemical sector, on the other hand, the projected privatisation is taking more time than was initially anticipated, because of technical difficulties encountered as well as political resistance. A new strategy was defined at the end of 1996 to take into account these obstacles, and the legal framework was revised accordingly; it identifies the secondary petrochemicals which can be produced privately, while clarifying the principles for private (and foreign) investment in the sector. Except for eight listed petrochemical products, all oil derivatives can be privately produced. For existing plants which are to be regrouped into saleable units, private investment will be allowed up to 49 per cent of the capital, the Mexican government keeping a majority share holding. On the other hand, private and foreign ownership is permitted up to 100 per cent in new plants, and the approval process for start-ups has been shortened.

Revenue from the current round of privatisation and from selling off concessions is not expected to be large compared with proceeds from the previous round (a cumulated amount of US$2.9 billion from 1995 up to November 1997, against US$24.7 billion in 1988-94). Resources obtained in the first round were used predominantly to repay foreign debt. The current government initially intended to create a development fund for infrastructure, but the project was abandoned in the aftermath of the 1994/95 crisis, and there is at present no earmarked use of revenue. In the case of railroads, as noted above, part of the revenue has been set aside to secure workers pension rights

The private sector is being increasingly involved in building-up infrastructure in the areas of communications and transport, water, natural gas, electricity, with the aim of raising both the volume of investment and the efficiency of its use. Private participation occurs in two modes: direct investment, where concessions are being granted (including Building-Operation-Transfer schemes, BOT); and a more indirect involvement – as defined in the budget for 1997 – whereby projects decided by the government are built by private firms, to be transferred back to the public sector upon completion. Such projects concern mainly the electricity sector and PEMEX where many investment projects are expected to generate large marginal revenues, which can then be used to pay for the acquisition of the project from the private investor without additional net claims on the budget. All in all, private infrastructure investment under these various schemes, together with increased public capital formation in key areas, should allow a catch-up on the delays accumulated over past years and contribute to the modernisation and capacity widening of the country's physical infrastructure, despite current budget tightness.

Regulatory and administrative reforms

Related to the privatisation process, Mexico's regulatory reform programme has made significant advances in 1997 regarding a number of areas such as natural gas, telecommunications, mining, railroads, transportation and environment. Over 60 legislative and administrative proposals have been reviewed and improved by the Economic Deregulation Council in several of these areas. Furthermore, it is now a legal requirement for all such proposals to be submitted to the Council along with a regulatory impact statement. All state governments have begun implementation of their respective regulatory reform programmes, and many are working together with the federal government to enhance regulatory harmonisation.

Although they have drawn less attention from the public, there have also been significant administrative reforms in a number of areas.

- The simplification of bureaucratic red tape affecting small and medium size enterprises (SMEs) which began in 1996 continued in 1997, reducing administrative obstacles to the creation and operation of enterprises.[53]
- To better meet development needs in the current context of budget restraint, the authorities have continued efforts to increase the effectiveness of public spending. Whereas performance was measured by inputs until now (*i.e.* resources spent), micro-indicators of performance are being developed. Budget procedures have also been modernised, with the installation of an on-line payment system for allocating funds across various Ministries.
- An autonomous tax collection agency (SAT) was created in 1997, as a separate body from the Ministry of Finance, in charge of tax collection and controls. In the future, it is envisaged to integrate SAT information records with those of IMSS. This year, already, with the social security reform, IMSS records were fully integrated with those of INFONAVIT, and all social security contributions are paid through a unified payment system. Modernising tax administration is important in a country like Mexico where tax evasion and/or tax avoidance is widespread. Reducing the under-declaration of income will raise tax revenue by widening the effective tax base and without increasing marginal tax rates that distort incentives. To serve this purpose, it may be desirable to review the tax system more generally. Mexico has one of the lowest tax revenue as percentage of GDP in the OECD, putting a tight constraint on public spending (Figure 13).

As recognised by the government (*Plan Nacional de Desarrollo 1995-2000*), some of the most urgent areas for reform to facilitate high sustainable growth over the medium and long term transcend the confines of narrowly-defined economic policy. Important changes have already taken place: for the first time since its creation in 1946 the ruling party lost its absolute majority in the lower house of parliament in the mid-1997 elections, considered to be one of the least controversial in Mexican History. This will help to strengthen institutional checks and balances, and the calm response of financial markets suggests that the business community at home and abroad welcomes the political change. And there is also urgent need for reform in the areas of internal security (police) and the judiciary system. The World Bank's 1997 *World Development Report*

Figure 13. **TAX/GDP RATIOS AND GDP PER CAPITA,1995-96**

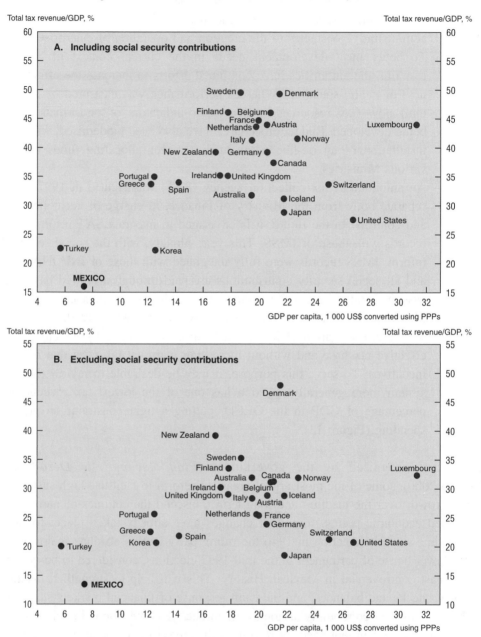

Source: OECD, *Revenue statistics of OECD Member countries* and *National accounts.*

discusses in some detail the efficiency losses and adverse distributive effects that can result from arbitrary state action and lack of good governance; their social costs are considerable and call for reform, which is indeed recognised as a priority by the current government.

Issues and developments in the banking sector

The Mexican financial system is in the midst of an adjustment process as the economy recovers from the 1995 crisis. The cost of the government's bank and debtor support programmes will affect public finances for years to come and is likely to act as a constraint on spending in other areas. The ultimate cost of these operations remains subject to some uncertainty. Apart from the fiscal cost of the banking crisis, there is a potential output loss as the over-indebtedness problems of firms and households have not been fully resolved. However, the economic recovery underway will help firms and households to grow out of their over-indebtedness problems. Widespread restructuring is taking place in the context of economy-wide structural changes. Among these, notably the reform of the pension system and an enhanced competitive environment should encourage growth of financial saving and efficiency in financial intermediation. For this potential to materialise, the non-performing loans problem must be surmounted, and incentive structures and supervisory mechanisms must be reinforced.

Banks' position improves

Capitalisation and reserves of the banking system have improved (Table 17). The doubling of the recorded non-performing loans in the first months of 1997 is explained by changes in accounting rules, to bring them into line with internationally accepted accounting principles.[54] The level of reserves in relation to non-performing loans has improved and the pressure for provisioning should ease somewhat. Growth of non-performing loans has been moderate following the change in accounting methods. Nevertheless, the scope for banks to accumulate profits is being reduced by increased competition (see below). For the portfolio of commercial and consumer credits, regulators expect that the full extent of the problem is already reflected in banks' mid-year financial statements. For mortgage loans, however, problems persisted up to mid-year when banks designed individual programmes to offer additional relief to their debtors. The effect of

Table 17. **Banking system indicators**

Per cent

	Dec. 1994	Dec. 1995	Dec. 1996	Jan. 1997	Sep. 1997
Total, banks in "normal situation"					
Capitalisation ratio	9.8	12.1	13.2	13.9	16.9
Non-performing loans					
(as share of total loans)	7.3	6.9	5.8	12.2[1]	13.1
Provisions					
(as share of non-performing loans)	48.6	72.6	119.9	58.7[1]	57.1
Memorandum items:					
Total, including FOBAPROA					
Capitalisation ratio	9.3	7.2	7.7	6.9	..
Non-performing loans					
(as share of total loans)	9.0	16.9	18.8	35.4[1]	..
Provisions					
(as share of non-performing loans)	43.3	54.1	74.4	37.7[1]	..

Note: Banks in "normal" situation: data in this category exclude the balance sheets of banks that have been placed under control of the authorities, excluding also the assets that have been transfered to FOBAPROA. Data reflect the situation of privately-owned banks after the clean-up.
Total including FOBAPROA: data include the balance sheets of those banks under control of authorities and the bank assets that have been sold to FOBAPROA by banks in "normal" situation. As from January 1997, indicators reported for the banking system refer to banks in "normal" situation only.

1. Data reflect the transition to the new accounting system (based on internationally accepted accounting principles).
Source: National Banking and Security Commission (CNBV).

these programmes should be known by December 1997. A remaining concern is that some of the loans that have already been restructured are still not serviced regularly, and part of this portfolio may yet again turn delinquent. However, authorities do not expect that this problem will be significant because of the long-term discounts on debt service provided by the different debt relief programmes and the recovery of real disposable income.

Support programmes to banks and debtors

Related government programmes (as described in the 1996 Mexico survey) comprise the following: take-over of poorly capitalised or badly managed banks ("intervened"); measures to strengthen banks not taken over ("not intervened"); and debtor support programmes. As a result of these programmes, FOBAPROA (which is the institution responsible for the protection of bank deposits) now controls over 36 per cent of the total stock of bank loans and about 31 per cent of total bank assets (Table 18). It acquired most of these bank assets between

Table 18. **Assets and loans held by banks and by FOBAPROA**

As of September 1997

	Assets		Loans	
	Billion pesos	%	Billion pesos	%
TOTAL	1 151	100	885	100
FOBAPROA	363	31.5	320	36.2
Loans purchased	303	26.3	270	30.5
Banks under control of authorities	60	5.2	50	5.6
Privately Mexican controlled	653	56.7	489	55.3
of which:				
Banks with foreign partner	368	32.0	277	31.4
New banks	38	3.3	27	3.0
Banks with foreign majority	135	11.7	76	8.6
of which: Acquisitions by foreign banks	94	8.1	60	6.7

Note: FOBAPROA's liabilities issued in the context of the bank support programme have been excluded from bank assets in the consolidation of the banking system accounts (including FOBAPROA).
Source: National Banking and Security Commission (CNBV).

1994 and 1996, as a result of: *i)* official interventions to take control of 13 banks (one was intervened in 1997) that were poorly capitalised or badly managed;[55] and *ii)* the loan purchase mechanism.

Measures to improve capitalisation include temporary measures (the PROCAPTE programme) and a programme to promote permanent capitalisation (FOBAPROA loan purchases). During 1995, support was granted to five banks under PROCAPTE in the form of subordinated convertible loans. The number of banks participating in the programme was reduced to two in 1996, and in early 1997 the programme was terminated.[56] The government has taken steps to support permanent capitalisation of banks by means of loan purchases through FOBAPROA (Box 3). These purchases have had no effect on the monetary base as banks received a government bond as payment. In order to qualify for this type of support, shareholders must increase the bank's capital.[57] The government expects that operations to promote permanent capitalisation came to an end with the operations that were carried out in 1996, some of which were formalised in 1997.

Debtor support programmes have provided incentives for debt restructuring and for debtors to stay current on debt payments. The federal government and the

Box 3. **FOBAPROA asset purchases from banks**

The loan purchases by FOBAPROA are in fact a swap in which the flows on a government bond are exchanged for the flows on a part of the banks' loan portfolio. This operation has been carried out by means of a trust that holds as claims any flows on the bank loans and as its main liability the obligation to repurchase the government bond that is held by the bank. This operation is to unravel in 10 years' time, at the latest, with the maturing of the government bond. Any revenue on the loan portfolio will be used to service the bond, and any excess value of the loan portfolio relative to that of the government bond will accrue to the bank. In case there is a shortfall between the value recovered from the loans and that of the bond, the loss will be shared by the government and the bank. Loss-sharing provisions vary: initial transactions set the banks' share in eventual losses at some 20 per cent, while more recent ones have higher loss sharing values (30 per cent).

The banks remain responsible for collecting interest on, and recovery of, the loans sold to FOBAPROA. Several incentives have been created for banks to adequately fulfill this role. First, banks can "re-purchase" their loans. Technically, any value outstanding in the trust (excess value of the loans relative to the bond banks have received from FOBAPROA) belongs to the bank. Second, a higher recovery rate on the loans will lessen their eventual payment under the loss-sharing rules. Third, they benefit from increased liquidity as soon as they can unravel the operation with FOBAPROA since the government bond is not a tradable asset. Fourth, the rate paid on the government bond is lower than the funding cost of the bank, thus there is a cost of carrying the position that the bank must fund.

In some cases, FOBAPROA asset purchases have in fact been one element in a procedure of orderly close-down of institutions, in which FOBAPROA as shareholder of the bank takes steps to separate the "good" from the "bad" bank and to bring in new shareholders to take-over the "good" bank. This policy of orderly bank close-downs was followed to avoid havoc in the system and contagion effects, as well as to maximise the re-sale value of the banks concerned. However FOBAPROA has been careful to establish adequate market signals in that its claims on bank assets come ahead of those of other shareholders and of subordinated debt issues.

banks share the costs of discounts on principal and interest payments offered to debtors that agree to restructure under the terms of the support programme. To qualify for the programme debtors must remain current on their debt service. While the UDI (Units of Investment) restructuring programme[58] constitutes the bulk of the fiscal cost of debtor support programmes, there are also a number of programmes that target specific groups of debtors. The programme to support small debtors (ADE), which provided an interest rate subsidy, was ended, and its fiscal cost has been paid in full. The size of other programmes increases as additional restructuring negotiations between parties are concluded, but the scope for further increases is limited given the already high participation rates. However, in some cases, coverage has been expanded or additional debt relief has been granted for target groups that continued to experience difficulty in servicing debts. In May 1997, the federal government provided additional funding of 10 billion UDIs to finance additional restructuring of mortgage loans. (This complementary programme was introduced in May 1996 to provide additional debt relief to home-owners that had already adhered to the UDI restructuring scheme but continued to experience debt servicing difficulties as debt burdens increased). Participation in the FINAPE (for agriculture and fisheries) and FOPYME (for small and medium-sized enterprises) programmes has also continued to expand,[59] promoting a normalisation of debt service on these loans. In addition, in the first half of 1997 the federal government introduced a programme to grant debt relief and lengthen maturities on debts of state and local governments that had already been restructured under the original UDI programme.

Estimates prepared by the National Banking and Securities Commission (CNBV) in November 1997 put the fiscal cost of bank and debtor support packages at some 11.9 per cent of 1997 GDP in present value terms[60] (Table 19), which compares with a net public sector debt of 21.9 per cent of GDP in 1994 before the crisis erupted. Any estimate of the net market value of problem loans remains uncertain; more accurate estimation will be made possible once the economy is on a sustainable medium-term growth path. Authorities plan to proceed with the sale of assets in FOBAPROA's portfolio and several options are being examined.

The Mexican banking crisis underlines the crucial importance of clear regulations as well as strong supervision securing their enforcement. The wide-ranging government rescue operation has succeeded in preventing a collapse of the banking system, but has weakened the incentive structure: the extent of coverage provided by FOBAPROA risks creating the perception that the government could provide protection well beyond a minimal safety net for small-scale deposits. Thus an important step in order to strengthen market discipline would be a clarification of the coverage of FOBAPROA's guarantees in the future,

Table 19. **Fiscal cost of support programmes for banks and debtors**[1]

	Per cent of GDP
Debt restructuring in investment units (UDIs)	
Original UDI programme	0.9
Additional programme for mortgage restructuring	1.2
Agricultural and fishing sector programme (FINAPE)	0.5
Small and medium-sized firms support programme (FOPYME)	0.2
Support to small debtors (ADE)	0.2
Debtor support programmes	**3.0**
Loans purchases for capitalisation schemes	2.4
Bank interventions and direct FOBAPROA support[2]	5.9
Restructuring of toll roads	0.6
Bank support programmes	**8.9**
Total	**11.9**[3]

1. Estimates as of October 1997, calculated as per cent of 1997 estimated GDP (3 202 billion pesos).
2. Includes the cost of assuming liabilities of banks that have been put under administration of FOBAPROA.
3. An amount equivalent to 2.2 per cent of GDP is already reflected in public sector financial accounts (either it has been paid for – the ADE cost – or it is included in the public debt).
Source: Ministry of Finance.

perhaps moving towards a regime whereby only small investors' deposits would be promised full protection.

Entry of new players and an expanded foreign presence

The 1990 reform of the banking law and NAFTA implementation eased barriers to entry to the Mexican banking sector. Subsequent to these changes there was a wave of new entrants to the banking sector before the 1994/95 crisis erupted. The performance of these new entrants has been disparate as they faced the double challenge of being new and riding a period of acute market instability. Five of the new entrants are among the group of 12 banks that have been put under the control of the authorities. While turbulence following the crisis may have caused some initial hesitation, overall the crisis boosted foreign participation beyond expectations at the time NAFTA was drafted. In response, the authorities have eased restrictions on foreign bank entry (*inter alia* ceilings on foreign bank participation were raised; for more details see the 1996 *Economic Survey* on Mexico).

The entry of foreign banks has played a significant role in solving the capitalisation problem following the crisis. Some have entered as part of bank rescue operations as the government offered incentives to attract new shareholders. Take-overs and mergers have allowed some foreign banks to gain quickly an established position in the Mexican market, while others have preferred to set up new fully owned subsidiaries. Nearly two-thirds of total banking assets are held by banks with a substantial foreign participation and 15 per cent of total banking assets are held by banks with foreign majority ownership (foreign bank and foreign shareholder participation was nearly zero only five years ago). Besides capitalisation, new entrants have brought innovation and a useful competitive stimulus to the domestic market. The enhanced competition is a challenge to established banks that have inherited the burden of a large non-performing loan portfolio. This may help push down margins and force banks into offering services that up to now they have found only marginally attractive; this in turn will foster growth of market segments, such as the retail deposit market, that have so far remained relatively underdeveloped.

IV. The reform of the Mexican health care system

Over the past decades, the overall health status of the Mexican population has improved significantly, as indicated by falling infant mortality, increased life expectancy, and the reduced incidence of premature deaths due to "avoidable" diseases (Figure 14).[61] This improvement coincided with increasing urbanisation and the development of infrastructures – sewerage and clean water supply in particular – as well as better maternal education and nutrition and improved access to health care. However, comparison with other countries with similar income levels, in the OECD area and in Latin America, suggests that there is room for further improvement.

In Mexico, unlike the situation in most other OECD countries, health problems prevalent in higher income countries coexist with epidemiological characteristics of lower-income countries. While it is still facing a significant incidence of common infectious diseases, malnutrition and problems related to insufficient mother and infant care, Mexico's health care system will have to respond increasingly to the needs of a more urbanised and ageing population whose pathological profile demands more technology-intensive, hence costlier, services.[62] In addition, there are substantial disparities of health and social conditions within the country: health status differs greatly across income classes and across regions. The relatively wealthy Northern states and the Federal District have health outcomes close to OECD averages, while poorer regions, mainly in rural areas in the South, have many health problems characteristic of less developed countries (Figure 15). Hence the challenges to the Mexican health system are many:

- to extend coverage, particularly to the population of rural areas with no regular services;
- to address the epidemiological backlog, and reduce disparities in health status among regions;

Figure 14. **HEALTH OUTCOMES: INTERNATIONAL COMPARISON**

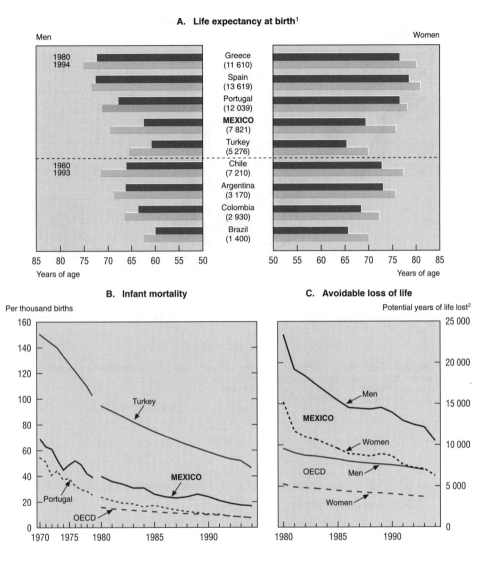

A. Life expectancy at birth[1]

Men · Women

B. Infant mortality

C. Avoidable loss of life

1. Figures in parentheses under the country name are GDP per capita for 1994 in purchasing power parities.
2. Rate per 100 000 male/female population, aged 0 to 69. These data, based on the "avoidable mortality" concept, provide a crude measure of premature mortality embracing both somatic and mental causes of death which could have been prevented if medical knowledge had been applied, if known public health principles had been in force, and if risky behaviour had not been so prevalent.

Source: Ministry of Health; OECD Health Database 1997; IDB.

Figure 15. **HEALTH STATUS BY REGIONS, 1994**

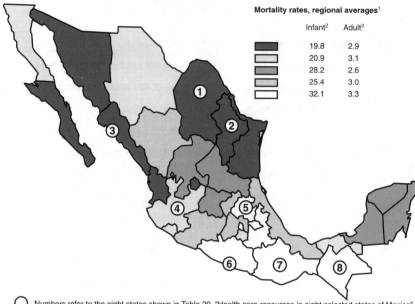

Mortality rates, regional averages[1]

	Infant[2]	Adult[3]
	19.8	2.9
	20.9	3.1
	28.2	2.6
	25.4	3.0
	32.1	3.3

(..) Numbers refer to the eight states shown in Table 20, "Health care resources in eight selected states of Mexico".

1. Regions regroup several states with similar health characteristics; averages are weighted by state population.
2. Infant deaths under one year per thousand live births.
3. Adult deaths per thousand inhabitants (aged 15 to 64 years).
Source: Ministry of Health; FUNSALUD (1994).

  – to respond to the different needs of a more urban population and higher income population groups;
  – to prepare for rising demand for quality health care related to rising incomes, democratisation and, increasingly, to ageing.

Faced with these challenges, the Mexican Government has undertaken reforms seeking to extend the coverage of health care and improve the quality of services. At the same time attention has been directed towards changes aimed at efficiency improvements. A comprehensive strategy to reform the health care system was outlined by the present administration in its National Development

Plan for 1995-2000 and more specifically the Programme for Health Sector Reform 1995-2000. Its implementation, which has started, will be carried out in successive phases over the medium term.

The present chapter first describes the main features of the existing Mexican health care system. After examining the problems of inequity, inefficiency and poor quality, key elements of the measures planned by the government as part of the reform strategy are discussed. Finally, the chapter evaluates the reform plans as to their likely effectiveness in addressing specific problems of the current health care system, and outlines concrete changes that have been undertaken, as well as those that remain to be made, to create a system which in the longer run is capable of meeting the challenges identified above.

The provision of heath care: a segmented system[63]

Mexico's health care system is divided into several vertically integrated segments, each covering a different population group (Box 4):

   i) various social security schemes, the largest of which is the Mexican Social Security Institute (IMSS), catering to insured workers in the formal sector;

   ii) the public health services provided by the Ministry of Health (SSA) for the population not covered by social security institutions;

   iii) a private sector that operates in an unsupervised environment.

Typically, the segments operate in parallel and do not formally compete with each other in the delivery of health care services. Moreover, there is a fundamental distinction between the institutions catering to the poor (who have no payment capacity) and those that provide services to households who have a capacity to pay (and often pre-pay, via insurance premia) for health care. The parallel subsystems that constitute the National Health System (excluding the private sector) are also vertically integrated, with each institution performing its own functions of financing and delivery of services to its target population.

Co-ordination between the various institutions in the National Health System has typically been low. The SSA and the different social security institutions maintain their own independent networks of primary level doctors and clinics as well as second and third level hospitals; the SSA also runs high-quality institutes

Box 4. Organisation of Mexican health care

The largest provider of health care is the public health system (also called the National Health System), which is divided into a social insurance segment and Ministry of Health (SSA) facilities, which typically perform a public assistance function:

i) Workers in the formal sector of the economy must be affiliated to one of several social security institutions: IMSS (the general scheme for employees and self-employed in the formal economy), ISSSTE (for civil servants, including the federal institute and six state institutes), PEMEX for its employees, two institutions for the armed forces (SEDENA for the Army and Air Force, MARINA for the Navy), covering 48 million people in all (SSA estimates for 1997).[1] The self-employed and workers in the informal economy have the option to affiliate to IMSS on a voluntary basis, but in practice, voluntary affiliation has remained low.

ii) The uninsured population (or ''open'' population), which is a heterogeneous group including people from rural areas and some marginal urban zones, has access to public health services provided by SSA either directly or through state health services; by IMSS-Solidaridad (public assistance funded by the federal budget and administered by the IMSS); and by the Department of the Federal District (DDF) in Mexico City; this group in total comprises roughly 34 million people[2] (Figure 16).

There is also a small private sector providing services of varying quality to individuals from all income categories. At one end of the spectrum, people from the higher-income brackets are the most likely to use private services, sometimes with funding from private insurance plans, but these, although expanding, still have a small coverage (officially estimated to be around 3.6 million people in 1996, less than 5 per cent of the population).[3] The poor and the very poor at the other end of the spectrum, and increasingly people in the middle-income brackets, also use private medical services, for which they usually pay out of pocket. The use of private health care is difficult to quantify precisely, but it may account for as much as 33 per cent of medical consultations for low income groups (SSA, 1994). Managed care organisations are still in their infancy.

---

1. In addition to health and maternity insurance, social security institutions provide a number of social benefits and services (pension, occupational risk coverage, child-care services, supermarkets, holiday resorts, etc.).
2. The figure refers to actual users of the services, whereas the number of potential users would be significantly higher. People using health services provided by the National Institute for Indigenous people (INI) in indigenous communities, and the Integrated Family Development Programme (DIF) for vulnerable groups are also included. Uninsured self-employed and workers in the informal sector, although they are legally entitled to use public health facilities, are not included here if they have a payment capacity and use private health care.
3. According to the 1994 National Health Survey, half of the people who subscribe to a private health insurance are also covered through the IMSS. In some cases private insurance is offered by employers as a complement to IMSS insurance; in a more limited number of cases, *e.g.* in the banking sector, companies have been allowed to opt out of the IMSS scheme, recovering part of their contribution to the IMSS *(reversión de cuota).*

(continued on next page)

(continued)

Figure 16. **THE MEXICAN HEALTH CARE SYSTEM**

Pre-Reform

Functions \ Population category	Insured population				Uninsured population		
	Private insurers	Social security systems			With access to public health services		No access
Regulation (Standardisation, quality control)	Commercial enterprises	IMSS	ISSSTE[1]	Others (PEMEX, Military, etc.)	SSA[2]	IMSS-Solidaridad	(Traditional medicine)
Financing (Insurance contributions or fee for service)	Commercial enterprises	IMSS	ISSSTE[1]	Others (PEMEX, Military, etc.)	SSA[2]	IMSS-Solidaridad	(Traditional medicine)
Service provision (Health care delivery)	Commercial enterprises	IMSS	ISSSTE[1]	Others (PEMEX, Military, etc.)	SSA[2]	IMSS-Solidaridad	(Traditional medicine)
Percentage of population covered (1996)[3]	3	49			41		7[4]

Higher income ⟶ **Lower income**

Note: IMSS: Mexican social security institute.
ISSSTE: Social security institute for civil servants.
SSA: Ministry of Health.
IMSS-Solidaridad: Public health services for poor rural communities.

1. Federal and state-level institutes.
2. Including state health services in decentralised states and Federal District health services.
3. For the uninsured population, the data refer to the legal coverage of the social security systems, while for public health services estimates are based on actual usage (in theory the entire uninsured population is covered by SSA services). In all the categories there is occasional recourse to private medical services without-of-pocket payment.
4. Some of the 10 million people who had no access to health care services in 1994 were reached by the programme of delivery of essential health care services that started in 1996 (see text).

Source: Ministry of Health.

of specialised care; each sector relies on salaried medical staff and operates its clinics and hospitals under global annual budgets. Under the different schemes of the National Health System, patients typically do not have the choice of general practitioner. There is no established procedure to refer patients from one scheme to another. In practice, however, patients under one social security institution are occasionally referred to facilities of another one or to the SSA's specialised institutes (or to private providers). This is done primarily when capacity or specialisation is lacking at the initial contact institution; increasingly it is also done for cost-effectiveness considerations.

Main problems under the pre-reform system

Inequity

To improve equity in the provision of health services is an explicit goal of the reform strategy pursued by the Mexican government. Although in theory the configuration of the health sector should ensure universal coverage of the population either through the social security system or government facilities, in reality a significant subset of the population – about 10 million Mexicans according to official estimates for 1994 – have little or no access to public health care.

The allocation of health care spending by institutions shows a strong bias in favour of the insured population (Figure 17). Social security schemes altogether cater to about half of the population, but account for 70 per cent of total health care expenditure (excluding private spending). The IMSS spends at least three times per capita for its clientele what the public assistance sector does for the uncovered population (measured on the basis of actual users). This allocation, given the government's participation in the IMSS budget, is not consistent with the stated objective of equitable distribution of government resources. The violation of this principle is even more pronounced when comparing the spending on health care for PEMEX workers and their dependants, which is the highest in per capita terms, with that of per capita spending by other public health care institutions.

The notion that social security schemes cater to the middle class and that private services are mainly used by upper income categories, thereby liberating public resources for the poor, is not fully supported by actual utilisation data. The

94

Figure 17. **PER CAPITA SPENDING BY PUBLIC HEALTH CARE INSTITUTIONS**

1995, National average = 100

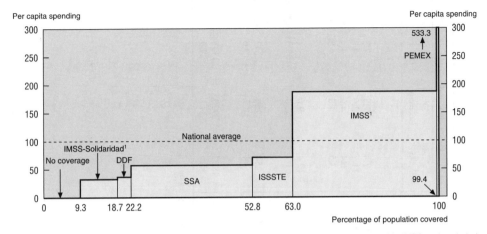

1. As the administrative support of IMSS-Solidaridad is provided by IMSS, its cost is recorded in IMSS and excluded from IMSS-Solidaridad.
Source: Ministry of Health.

actual behaviour of the population does not match the market segmentation and there are overlapping demands: some social security beneficiaries have recourse to private medical services or to Ministry of Health services (directly or at state level), even though this entails multiple payments by the consumer in many cases. Spending on private care by low-income households is not negligible either: according to national survey results, as many as 9 per cent of low-income households use private medical care, compared with 10 per cent for middle-income households (INEGI, 1994). As a proportion of their income, poor households spend more than the middle- and high-income groups, 5 per cent for households in the two lower deciles, against 3 per cent for households in the upper half of the income distribution. Such out-of-pocket payment for private care adds to problems of inequity.

The uncovered population is concentrated in certain regions, because of geographic isolation or of deficient delivery of services.[64] In each segment of the National Health System – social security and government facilities alike – the distribution of financial resources is rather unequal between states. Despite

95

Table 20. **Health care resources in eight selected states of Mexico**[1]

	Northern States			Pacific region	Poorer states in the South and interior			
	1 Coahuila	2 Nuevo León	3 Sinaloa	4 Jalisco	5 Puebla	6 Guerrero	7 Oaxaca	8 Chiapas
Physical and human resources per 10 000 inhabitants								
Doctors	13.9	12.9	10.7	10.5	7.4	7.8	7.8	7.8
Nurses	26.3	25.8	20.1	18.5	11.7	12.6	10.8	11.0
Hospital beds	11.5	10.8	8.1	9.7	6.4	4.6	4.4	4.1
Consultation units	5.7	5.6	5.0	4.5	3.5	4.8	4.5	4.3
Utilisation indicators								
Daily consultations per general practitioner	13.3	15.6	15.9	13.6	12.4	9.6	9.1	8.8
Average bed occupancy (%)	66.5	77.7	77.1	53.3	61.1	62.8	65.3	67.6
Public spending per capita[2]								
Total (pesos)	616	680	470	408	254	256	242	250
of which: Preventive care (%)	5.1	4.5	7.7	4.6	7.4	8.2	13.6	12.1
Memorandum items:								
Population (thousands)	2179	3458	2383	6173	4807	2978	3375	3686
of which: Covered by social security (%)	75.4	72.1	58.1	49.2	33.3	34.1	24.4	23.5

1. 1995 data, numbers above the columns refer to the map in Figure 15 which shows health status indicators by region.
2. Spending by social security institutions and public health care providers only.
Source: Ministry of Health.

substantial public investment in the poorer states over recent years, these states still receive significantly less resources per capita from the SSA budget than the national average, even though the incidence of disease is much above the national average. Until the reform, budget allocation to the states did not take into account the health needs, poverty and access conditions nor the revenue generating capacity of each state; and in fact, states with the highest tax revenue per capita were receiving the highest resources per capita from the Federal Government. In the social security system, also, the lowest per capita health spending is recorded in states where needs for health care are the highest (Table 20).

Low quality services and inefficiency

Some of the deficiencies in health care may have resulted from the drastic budget cuts over the period 1982-88. Despite an increase in health spending in the following years and the concomitant improvement in SSA services, a significant segment of the population still considered Mexico's health services as unsatisfactory according to survey results for 1994 (SSA, 1994). The most frequently cited problem was the poor quality of services and the lack of resources. Deficiencies in infrastructure, lack of trained health professionals and poor supervision are the quality problems most often mentioned. A related source of dissatisfaction among users of public sector health services is long waiting times – survey results indicate that patients wait on average 60 minutes prior to obtaining care in social security facilities and 43 minutes in SSA facilities, while average waiting time for private care is 17 minutes. Travel time to access health facilities is an additional factor that can discourage the use of health services, even in urban areas: total time cost for medical care (including travel time) is again higher for social security services than for SSA facilities.[65] Because health facilities in several states are in poor condition, some low income households, who in principle are covered by SSA services, go without medical attention or have recourse to private services at their own expense. Lack of medication in public health clinics is often cited as a reason for using alternative services. At the same time, insufficient co-ordination within the National Health System is responsible for duplication of services, especially in urban areas. Even in smaller towns and rural areas, there is evidence of duplication of public assistance services, because of insufficient co-ordination (between IMSS-Solidaridad hospitals and SSA hospitals, for instance), despite the scarcity of public resources in general.

In 1994, Mexico spent the equivalent of 5-6.5 per cent of GDP on health care, depending on the estimate (Box 5).[66] The ratio for other OECD countries with similar income levels – Greece, Turkey – falls within this range (Figure 18). While most experts agree that the public component of spending (2.6 per cent of GDP in 1994) is low by international standards, estimates of private health expenditure are subject to considerable uncertainty, related in particular to private practice of public sector doctors. Per capita health expenditure in Mexico was among the lowest in the OECD area, in accordance with the relative position of Mexico's GDP per capita. In comparison to other Latin American countries (Argentina, Brazil, Chile, Colombia), health spending in Mexico (both total and the public component) is close to what is expected in relation to the country's overall GDP and per capita income (IADB, 1996). The main problem in Mexico is not so much low health care spending as such, but rather the fact that a ''normal'' level of spending is associated with large unmet needs (e.g. incomplete coverage). Additional problems are related to regional disparities and the inadequate allocation of resources by programmes.

Within the constraints imposed on government spending for budget control purposes, the authorities have sought to provide the uncovered population at large with health services which are known to be the most cost-effective to reduce morbidity and mortality. The breakdown of health spending by programme shows that 50 per cent of public health expenditure is on curative care delivered in hospitals, 25 per cent on administration, and 11 per cent on preventive care (Figure 19). The proportion of spending on prevention appears to be inadequate in view of what is recommended by international experts for countries in the same income category – although due to the budget structure there are some preventive actions budgeted under curative care. The Mexican authorities themselves have recognised that the cost-effectiveness of public expenditure needs to be improved.[67] On a state by state basis, however, the allocation of public resources by programme appears less inadequate. Even though total health care spending per capita is lower in poorer states than in richer ones, the proportion of total spending allocated to preventive care is much higher than in richer states, in accordance with the requirements of the specific epidemiological characteristics of poor states, where only a minority of the population is covered

Box 5. **Financing health care**

The ratio of health spending to GDP declined by more than 1 percentage point between 1982 and 1988 (on Ministry of Finance estimates) - largely a consequence of the decline in households' real income following the 1982 debt crisis and budget cuts related to public finance consolidation. Since 1988, however, spending on health care has recovered, and by 1992 the ratio to GDP was back to the pre-debt crisis level. Although the 1995 economic recession led again to a decline in total spending, it is expected that in 1997 the ratio will be higher than that of 1992.

The increase of health spending relative to GDP in 1988-94 reflects a larger allocation of public funds as well as increased financing from other sources. Health care prices, which moved broadly in line with the consumer price index until 1989, increased steadily in the early 1990s relative to the general price level.[1]

Public health care is financed for the most part through payroll taxes and subsidies from the central government. Social security institutions, which provide health care to affiliates and dependants, are financed by compulsory contributions from employers and employees, with a complement from the general budget.[2] The increase in contribution rates, starting in the late 1980s, to strengthen the financing of the health component of IMSS is likely to have constrained the expansion of the formal economy and induced under-declaration of earnings (IMSS, 1996). Public health services for the ''open'' population are financed by general taxation.

Other sources contribute in a much smaller, but rising, proportion to the financing of health care. Health services provided in SSA facilities and in state hospitals charge user fees, in principle proportional to patients' payment capacity: revenue from these fees has doubled to about 10 per cent of total SSA spending in 1994 (from below 5 per cent in the early 1980s). State government contributions, which were negligible 15 years ago, have been increasing over the years: depending on the state, they accounted for 5 to 15 per cent of health care spending at the state level in 1994. States' own revenues are kept by the state, but their use has so far been highly regulated by the central government. The IMSS-Solidaridad programme is mostly financed from federal funds, the IMSS providing administrative and technical support, which is estimated to amount to some 10 per cent of federal funding. Private health service payments are in general not reimbursed (private insurance coverage is small), but there is an indirect subsidy as these payments are tax deductible – a system which is not capped and benefits higher-income families more than others. All in all, the government's coverage of total health care costs has been estimated at 21 per cent, business contributions at 30 per cent, while household income accounts for the largest share (49 per cent) through contributions to IMSS, out-of-pocket payments and private insurance premiums (Ministry of Finance).

---

1. Based on the ''Health care'' component of the CPI (Bank of Mexico) covering medical services, pharmaceuticals and other medical products. The price of medical services fell during most of the 1980s relative to the CPI, reflecting real wage cuts of the medical staff. There was some catching up in 1989-94, but this trend was reversed again in 1995-96. Relative prices of pharmaceuticals, after declining in the later part of the 1980s, have caught-up over the past few years, as price controls were relaxed.
2. The health component of the IMSS (Sickness and Maternity Insurance) has always run a deficit, but as accounts were indistinct, this deficit was effectively covered by contributions to the IMSS Old Age Insurance component – permanently in surplus until recently because of the age structure of the insured population.

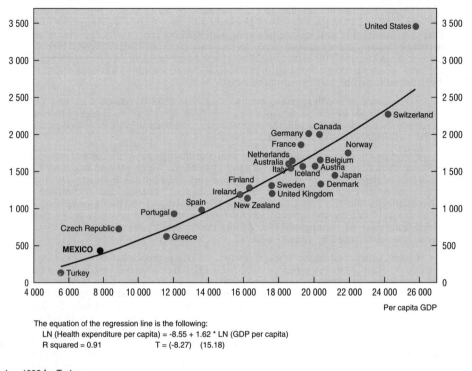

Figure 18. **HEALTH EXPENDITURE AND GDP PER CAPITA**
US dollars, converted using PPP's, 1994[1]

The equation of the regression line is the following:
LN (Health expenditure per capita) = -8.55 + 1.62 * LN (GDP per capita)
R squared = 0.91   T = (-8.27)   (15.18)

1.   1993 for Turkey.
Source: OECD Health Data 1997; FUNSALUD.

by social security, so that the public sector plays a predominant role in providing health care (Table 20, *Memorandum item*).

Some of the observed deficiencies are clearly due to the absence of well designed incentives in a system whose institutional structure has developed historically. As the Mexican health care system combines features of two polar models – a "public integrated model" and a "private contract model" – it suffers from some of the disadvantages of these two models.[68] On the one hand, the system exhibits many of the shortcomings characteristic of the "public integrated model": both segments of the National Health System – Ministry of

Figure 19. **ALLOCATION OF HEALTH CARE BUDGET BY PROGRAMME**
Per cent of total

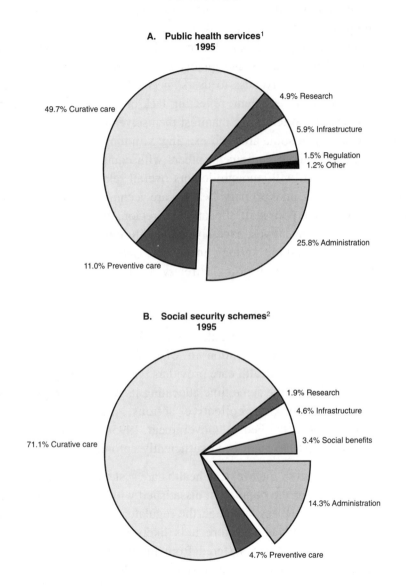

A. Public health services[1]
1995

49.7% Curative care

4.9% Research

5.9% Infrastructure

1.5% Regulation
1.2% Other

25.8% Administration

11.0% Preventive care

B. Social security schemes[2]
1995

71.1% Curative care

1.9% Research

4.6% Infrastructure

3.4% Social benefits

14.3% Administration

4.7% Preventive care

1. Including SSA, DDF, IMSS-Solidaridad.
2. Based on IMSS and ISSSTE; the breakdown is not available for PEMEX.
Source: Ministry of Health.

101

Health (SSA) and social security schemes – exercise quasi-monopoly power over their clientele, with no effective consumer choice. Since the provider of services is also the regulator, the degree of supervision and quality control is erratic because of frequent conflicts of interests. In the absence of proper incentives for good performance of the providers and with regulation enforced through a "command and control" mode, costs and quality control are unsatisfactory, and the system shows little responsiveness to users' needs.[69] In addition, allocation of resources has often been inefficient, reflecting lack of management capacities at the local level. These shortcomings manifest themselves in various ways: under-utilisation of capacity in some areas co-existing with too little capacity in others (there are hospitals without equipment, others with equipment but no doctors); inadequate mix of staff, with enough doctors overall relative to the population, but not enough nurses and primary health care technicians;[70] absenteeism of health professionals and poor staff allocation by region, due to inadequate supervision and the lack of incentives; excessive expenditure on drugs, in part reflecting an inefficient distribution system; inadequate patient referral, patients by-passing first level care and going directly to more costly second-level institutions.[71]

Because of the dilution of the responsibilities of the Ministry of Health, which was increasingly providing health care directly to the non-insured, it was not able to devote sufficient attention to what should be its essential role: monitoring, regulating other health care providers, and establishing standards for the entire system, while at the same time allocating its resources to public health policies *per se* (undertaking collective actions, preventive information campaigns, vaccinations, etc.; Federal Government, 1995*b*). Furthermore, regulations where they existed have not been sufficiently enforced.

The private segment of the Mexican health care system has played a complementary role, catering for the population dissatisfied with the services offered by the public system. Nonetheless, although the regulatory framework exists, there is sufficient enforcement and therefore it is likely that private financing and provision of services have also suffered from inefficiencies. The diversity of financing and delivery entities in the private sector has resulted in segmented markets where service providers could exploit consumers because of asymmetry of information, and insurers could "cream-skim" the population with low medical risks.[72]

The reform of the health care system

With a view to providing high-quality and cost-effective health care for the entire population, the present administration has outlined a reform strategy in its Development Plan. The specific reform programme for the health sector (*Programa de Reforma del Sector Salud, 1995-2000*) provides more details. The three major objectives of the on-going reform (stated more or less explicitly) are:

i) providing access to public health care to the population so far not covered;

ii) making provision of services for the entire population more efficient;

Figure 20. **THE MEXICAN HEALTH CARE SYSTEM: REFORM PROPOSAL**[1]

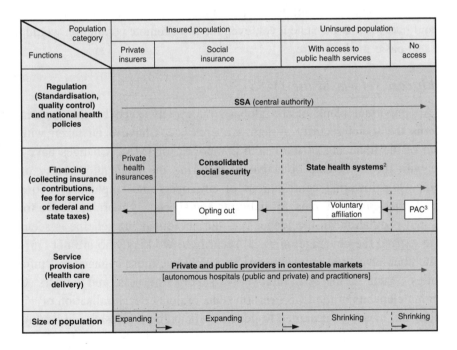

1. In the longer run.
2. Integrated with IMSS-Solidaridad.
3. Programme for extension of coverage.
Source: OECD Secretariat; national authorities.

iii) establishing a health care system that is not prone to automatic future explosion of expenditure.

This reform is a long-term endeavour, to be carried out in successive phases along several tracks. In some areas, measures have already been implemented; in others, precise actions to be taken have yet to be defined, while in other areas still, only the general direction of the desired changes has been indicated in the government's programme. In the longer run, when the reform is complete, the new system is to be organised more by functions, as illustrated by Figure 20, in a horizontal structure in stark contrast to the vertical segmentation of the present system (illustrated in Figure 16 above). Under the new model, the SSA is to concentrate its efforts on regulation and normative functions. Financing is to come from various sources (insurance contributions, service fees, federal and state taxes). There would be many providers (both public and private) competing to deliver services. The integrated social security sector is expected to cover a large share of the population; public assistance services would be fully decentralised and integrated at the state level; even the most remote population would have access to basic medical care.

Health care reform in the IMSS

An important plank of the global strategy envisaged by the government concerns the social security system. Concrete steps have been taken with the reform of the financing of the health component of IMSS. Changes have been made with the immediate objective of restoring the financial viability of the system, while lowering contributions of employers and employees – so as to reduce labour costs and make affiliation to social security more attractive for the uninsured population. In the longer run, the new financing scheme is seen as a way to expand the coverage of social security to workers who are not currently affiliated but have a pre-payment capacity (including those engaged in "informal activities", such as the self-employed in small businesses, and farmers. Other important elements of the IMSS reform – the regional decentralisation of administration and measures designed to generate competitive pressures in health care services (detailed below) – seek to improve quality and efficiency (IMSS, 1996).

The financing formula for Medical and Maternity Insurance has been significantly modified: the new modalities increase the share from general taxation, while reducing the share from payroll taxes. At the same time, marginal tax rates have been lowered to promote compliance and accurate declaration of earnings; and part of the contribution (employers' and the government's) is based on a fixed fee per worker (Box 6). The rationale for reducing payroll taxes, according to the authorities, is that high marginal rates induce a lower participation in formal employment by making it expensive to increase employment and wages as productivity increases. Given the large incidence of evasion from social security contributions,[73] lower payroll taxes with increased financing from general taxation should help bring into the system a significant proportion of the population currently working in the informal economy. A related argument is that financing standardised medical care through proportional (or progressive) payroll contributions makes the latter more like a tax rather than an insurance premium, entailing the customary distortions; and subsidies to the scheme can be justified by positive externalities of universal health insurance. The reform also introduces new options to make voluntary affiliation to IMSS less costly, thereby facilitating entry into the regime of households among the ''middle class'' and the ''near-poor'' who are currently not covered. In this case also, the government contributes a fixed sum per person insured.

Increasing the government's participation in the financing of social security is seen by the IMSS authorities as the counterpart to the bigger role the IMSS is to play in the transition phase of the government's strategy: the social security institute is to take on the responsibility of funding (and in the short-term supplying) standard health services to the quasi-totality of the urban population and in densely populated rural areas – social security thus becoming a minimum health insurance – while the public assistance sector remains in charge of delivering services to marginal populations (a narrower segment than at present). At the same time, the IMSS recognises that, as its coverage expands, control instruments, will be required to avoid excess demand for services, as well as a fiscal strategy to contain government spending in the longer run.

The new financing mechanisms are to be accompanied by a process of modernisation and decentralisation of IMSS, which is deemed necessary to improve the quality of services and to contain costs. Regional decentralisation started in 1995, when seven regional IMSS Directorates were created, each having 70 to 80 hospitals to monitor. The regional agencies are given more autonomy in decision making, so as to improve responsiveness to clients' needs, although not all decision making will be decentralised.[74] A formula has been

Box 6. **Reform of IMSS health fund financing**

Before the reform, the IMSS health fund was financed by contributions set at 12.5 per cent of wages, shared between employers (8.75 per cent), workers (3.125 per cent) and the federal government (0.625 per cent).

Under the *new financing scheme,* the government's monthly contribution is a fixed amount for each affiliated worker: 84 pesos of December 1995 (13.9 per cent of the minimum wage) indexed to the CPI.[1] Employers also contribute a fixed fee for each worker (set initially at 84 pesos also, indexed to the minimum wage).[2] A proportional contribution is added for income above three times the minimum wages – it is initially set at 8 per cent of the part of wages above 3 minimum wages, to be split between employers (75 per cent) and employees (25 per cent). Over the coming ten years, the employers' fixed fee will gradually increase, while the proportional employer-employee contribution will gradually decrease: at the end of the ten-year period, the employers' fixed fee will be 180 pesos (1997II prices), while the employer-employee contribution will be down to 1.5 per cent of income above three times the minimum wage (Figure 21). In addition to the above, a tripartite contribution is levied to finance additional economic benefits for maternity and sickness subsidies – 1 per cent of gross wages, to be split between employers (75 per cent), employees (20 per cent) and government (5 per cent).

Voluntary affiliation. The new options for voluntary affiliation to the IMSS obligatory regime (including health care insurance and pension) make a distinction between: *i)* the self-employed (such as peasants and shopkeepers...), for whom contributions are based on the minimum wage (13.9 per cent of one minimum wage, *i.e.* 112 pesos in 1997II); and *ii)* wage earners in special situations (such as domestic workers, and state employees) who will contribute in proportion to their wages. The Federal Government contributes the same fixed amount per capita in case of voluntary adherence as it does in the case of the obligatory registration.

Health insurance for the family. A new scheme is introduced which will provide medical insurance (but not the pension benefits) to households for a modest fixed contribution of 22.4 per cent of the minimum wage (180 pesos in 1997II).

---

1. This corresponds to 112 pesos during the second semester of 1997, equivalent to approximately US$14.
2. Indexing the government contribution to the CPI is seen as a way to protect this component from the effect of inflation; moreover it may constrain providers to maintain health care inflation in line with general inflation if the government's contribution is to remain constant in real terms. By indexing employers' contributions to the minimum wage rather than the CPI, the authorities intend to leave non-wage labour costs as flexible in real terms as the minimum wage (IMSS, 1996).

(continued on next page)

(continued)

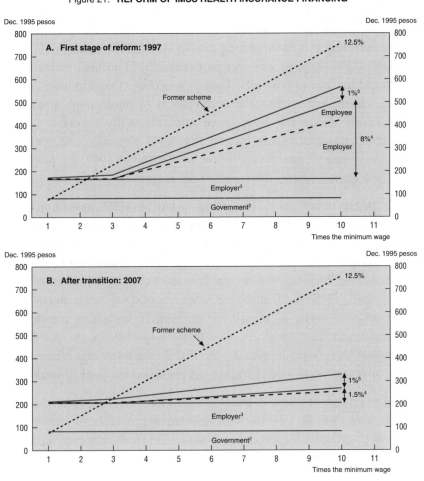

Figure 21. **REFORM OF IMSS HEALTH INSURANCE FINANCING**[1]

A. **First stage of reform: 1997**

Dec. 1995 pesos

12.5%

Former scheme

1%[5]

Employee

8%[4]

Employer

Employer[3]

Government[2]

Times the minimum wage

B. **After transition: 2007**

Dec. 1995 pesos

12.5%

Former scheme

1%[5]

1.5%[4]

Employer[3]

Government[2]

Times the minimum wage

1. See text for a detailed explanation.
2. Monthly contribution, equivalent to 13.9 per cent of the minimum wage in the Federal District (SMDF).
3. Equivalent to 13.9 per cent of the SMDF. The contribution increases progressively to 20.4 per cent in ten years time.
4. Proportional to the part of wages above 3 SMDF wages, split between employers and employees. Rate falls progressively to 1.5 per cent in 2007.
5. Tripartite contributions of 1 per cent of the gross wage, for additional economic benefits.
Source: IMSS.

designed to allocate resources to the regional agencies based on the needs of the population and independent of regional wage levels. In the ongoing debate to improve efficiency in service delivery by IMSS, out-sourcing of ancillary services in hospitals and allowing clients' free choice of family doctors have been considered. Selection of own primary care doctors, combined with giving these doctors a controlling and co-ordinating role for determining access to higher level care (acting as gatekeepers) was seen as potentially improving patients' referral to second- and third-level hospitals. The out-sourcing of certain hospital services has started. On the other hand, the development of pilot programmes to allow choice of family doctor has been slower than originally expected, because of concerns about the relative earnings of first level physician and specialists in secondary and tertiary units. Nevertheless, by the end of 1997, the programme is likely to have been tested in the seven IMSS regions.

IMSS began to reform its budgeting system in 1997, and further changes will be implemented in 1998. A risk-adjusted capitated formula is being used to develop the health budget considering the "medical zone" as a basic unit to allocate resources. There are 131 medical zones, each containing between one to three second-level hospitals and several first-level clinics, the so-called "Family medicine units". IMSS will introduce a system of Diagnostic Related Groups (DRG) to measure costs, as a main determinant of budgetary transfers across medical zones and from medical zones to third-level hospitals. As the largest provider of health services in Mexico, the IMSS sees a fair and efficient internal allocation of resources as key to improving results in the general health system.

Another important plank in the IMSS reform project concerns the development of a more flexible relation with alternative providers of health services. With a view to generating competitive pressures in the health care services so as to enhance the efficiency of operations and bring about better results in terms of fairness, the IMSS will seek to separate financial management of social security funds from its medical operations in such a way that allocation of resources to service providers is not based on past expenditure. This is seen as a way to improve resource allocation in the IMSS health system, and support a healthier mix of public and private supply of health services to the population covered by IMSS. For alternative suppliers (such as managed care organisations) it would mean the possibility of drawing resources from the social security funds to finance health services, subject to appropriate regulation. A principal objective of regulations associated with managed care organisations will be to protect the social security fund from undue financial risk by reducing the possibilities for opportunistic behaviour. Among other restrictions, the option would only be available to large companies as a whole and large groups, not individuals; minimum levels of capitalisation and quality standards as well as minimum periods of permanency in a health plan would be required; and special provisions to finance chronic illness would be used. Besides a strong regulatory framework, gradualism is also held as a strategic principle in proceeding with this aspect of health care reform.

This co-operation with managed care organisations replaces the general "opting out" facility with fee reimbursement which was envisaged earlier and in several ways resembled a mechanism that already existed on a small scale. Since its foundation in the early 1940s, the IMSS has operated a "fee reimbursement mechanism" (*reversión de cuotas*), by means of which employers receive a percentage (71.5 per cent in most cases) of the social security taxes in exchange for the provision of health services.[75] A review of the results of health reform programmes in OECD countries, Latin American countries and other regions, has demonstrated the high fiscal and social risks associated with breaking up the pool of risks managed by social security. Thus, the traditional fee reimbursement system is seen by the IMSS as likely to show undesirable results if expanded.

Ministry of Health decentralisation

Reforms in the Ministry of Health (SSA) and its delivery of health care services are at present proceeding in parallel to those in the IMSS. The focus of these reforms is to increase efficiency, while making changes that move the system towards the long-term model of national health care organisation outlined in Figure 6. Initial attempts to decentralise public health services were already undertaken in the period 1983-87, with 14 states receiving responsibility for health care delivery to the uninsured (until then under the SSA control), including in rural areas previously provided by IMSS-COPLAMAR, an institution that continued to operate as IMSS-Solidaridad in non-decentralised states. The process was essentially an administrative decentralisation, but states remained subject to both formal (regulatory and budgetary) and informal controls, with discretionary budget allocation and programmes decided at the national level.

Comparing outcomes in terms of quality of services and access of the poorest segments of the population in decentralised states with those of the other states over the period 1985-95 suggests that the main determinant of progress during the period was the relative situation of the states at the start of the decentralisation exercise, rather than decentralisation itself: states that did best were those with a greater administrative capacity and economic resources, enabling them to assume more financing responsibilities (from their own revenues) and to profit from the newly offered opportunities.[76] Some of the problems that emerged during the first decentralisation exercise, especially in the poorer states, highlight the need to establish proper tools – developing health indicators and defining a package of essential health care interventions – to help monitor spending effectiveness and to enhance local administrative capacity in line with decentralisation.

The renewed decentralisation efforts undertaken by the current administration affects all states. The National Health Council (*Consejo Nacional de Salud,* 1995) was established in 1995 to bring together health authorities from the federal and state governments in order to ensure co-ordination in the National Health System: it is to propose concerted actions, standardise evaluation procedures, develop technical co-operation between states, etc. After the signature of a national agreement between the federal government and state governments in 1996, each state elaborated a specific model of reform providing a diagnosis of the existing situation, defining objectives (to reorganise state health services and improve coverage of the uninsured population) and making specific proposals for action. By October 1997, 31 Agreements had been signed with the SSA, the Federal District and all but one state having participated. A new formula has been introduced, starting in 1996, to correct inequities in the allocation of federal transfers to states, with the explicit objective of narrowing the gap in available resources per person for health care between the richer states and the poorer ones. The formula is based on a poverty index, a measure of mortality (the standardised mortality ratio) and the size of the population (all indicative of the ''relative needs'' of the state); it also reflects the states' capacity to raise funds.[77]

The decentralisation seeks to delegate more decision power to the states, in particular concerning resource allocation. However, some investment decisions will continue to be made at the federal level. Part of the transfers to the states is earmarked, in particular those corresponding to the delivery of the basic package for the poor (see below). According to the new allocation of responsibilities, the Ministry of Health (SSA) reinforces its regulatory functions, establishing standards and quality controls, its role being enhanced as resources are freed to focus more on what should be its essential activities (SSA, 1996). To ensure that states allocate sufficient resources to basic health care previously provided by the SSA, a list of essential health care cost-effective programmes has been established for state health services to implement in conformity with national and international health objectives. The states are now evaluated according to a set of 71 health indicators that emphasise results concerning health outcomes and establish targets to be achieved by the year 2000. Thus, while the states are granted more flexibility in the use of resources, the SSA is strengthening its monitoring functions.

The decentralisation process is being implemented as follows:

i) The federal government has set up expert groups to assist states in strengthening their administrative capacity; these are to provide technical support for planning and budgeting, and to ensure that information flows between states and the national regulatory unit in the SSA.

ii) New public bodies have been created in the states (*organismos publicos de decentralizacion*, OPD): the budget for health is passed on to these bodies who will be given autonomy for making current expenditure decisions. Except for wages, which are set at the federal level, they can freely decide resource allocation across first and second level care.[78] Ministry of Health employees who work at the state level now become state employees (of OPDs); all state employees are to have a contract with the state, but negotiations (and settlements) on general working conditions and pay scale adjustments continue to take place at the federal level, between the national unions and the Ministry of Health.

iii) SSA services and IMSS-Solidaridad are to be integrated at the state level when IMSS-Solidaridad is decentralised. This planned integration is lagging due to difficulties arising in particular from differences in wage levels and working conditions between IMSS and state employees which explain resistance by trade unions.

Monitoring of states' activity is carried out at two levels: first, the state's Secretary of Health issues a yearly report on activity to the state's congress; second, the SSA requires states to report on the allocation of resources, achievements and the implementation of the essential health care programmes.

Extension of coverage

In the government's strategy, priority was given to the extension of coverage of basic health care, to be achieved in successive steps. Implementation of the first step is now well underway with the immediate introduction of a specific programme (*Programa de Ampliación de Cobertura, PAC*), to deliver a package of basic health services to the 10 million persons that were identified to have no regular access, in particular the 8 million located in the poorest and most sparsely populated areas of 18 states. The package – which is distinct from the essential health care programmes that decentralised states will have to provide to the uninsured population – comprises 12 basic health services, selected for their cost-effectiveness and targeted to groups in extreme poverty who previously had little or no access to health care. It is financed by ear-marked federal transfers to the states (the OPDs), who are responsible for operating the programme, but the ongoing reform provides for a margin of flexibility in the application of the package, according to the specific needs of the state. Almost 4 million people were covered by the programme in 1996; by September 1997, the number of beneficiaries had increased to 6 million (1997 State of the Union Report); and it is expected that almost 8 million persons will be covered by the year 2000. The remaining target population, located in more densely populated areas, will be covered in parallel through the decentralisation of public health services. By avoiding duplication, spending funds in ways that better match local needs and improving cost-effectiveness in the delivery of services, the decentralised states are expected to be able to meet the basic needs of the uninsured population in the less remote rural areas and in urban zones.

The financing reform of the IMSS health component – with the new modalities for voluntary affiliation – is also an important element of the strategy to extend the coverage of health services, as it seeks to enrol in the social security system people outside (or at the edge) of the formal sector, who have a capacity, albeit modest, to pay. Expanding the coverage of IMSS is desirable in its own right to improve equity in the health system; it is also seen as conducive to a better allocation of IMSS resources, with a shift towards more cost-effective interventions, because it would create the conditions for delivering preventive care to families on a permanent basis, while this is not possible at present when workers in the informal sector only join the IMSS when in need of curative treatment for serious illness. But several years are needed for the effects of the reform to materialise. According to official projections, the number of affiliates could grow by 3.5-4 per cent per year, *i.e.* 1.5-2 percentage points above labour force growth; as a result the coverage of the labour force by IMSS would exceed 40 per cent of the population in ten years' time (6 to 8 percentage points more than at present.)

Regulatory framework and arbitration

Under the framework of the new *Ley General de Salud* several measures have been taken with regard to deregulation, strengthening sanitary control, and expanding the availability of generic drugs in the private market. The effect of the latter has a direct impact on the out-of-pocket payments of the poorer segments of the population, thus alleviating in part inequities of the system; in addition it is an important tool for cost containment. It is expected that the generic market will gradually develop, beginning in 1998.

In order to resolve the conflicts that are generated in the practice of health care, the National Commission of Medical Arbitration (CONAMED) was established in June 1996. It is staffed by interdisciplinary professional health experts. Its objective is to analyse, evaluate and resolve the conflicts that could arise between providers and consumers of services. In its first year of operation, CONAMED received more than 4 000 requests, 84 per cent of which were resolved by conciliation.

Assessment of current reform efforts and what needs to be done

As discussed above, the pre-reform health care system was ill-adapted to meet the triple challenge of expanding the coverage, containing costs and ensuring services of high quality. OECD countries' experience suggests that there is no single ideal system of health care provision. Practices differ as to how health care services are financed and delivered, and how specific contractual arrangements between patients, service providers and payers are articulated. There is nonetheless consensus among health economists and experts that neither a centrally administered nor a purely market-based system produce the most desirable outcomes, and that an optimal system – which should provide every citizen guaranteed access to what is considered a minimum set of services – combines elements of appropriate government regulation and competitive mechanisms. Similarly there is consensus about the desirability of separating purchasers and providers.

Against this general background, the desirability of the stated long-term goal of the current reform project – moving away from a system in which the population's health care needs are looked after by parallel, vertically integrated sub-systems towards one which is organised according to key functions – seems indisputable. But many details of the future system remain to be spelt out, and current reform efforts continue to be confined within the existing framework of segmented coverage and risk pooling. Each of the main sub-systems in the health care system has its own reform plan and agenda. Large uncertainties surround some of the announced measures and there seems to remain different views about what the final outcome of the overall reform should be and how it can best be implemented. Specific reform measures currently being implemented or under consideration are assessed below with respect to their contribution to remedying existing problems as well as their possible role in moving the current system towards one which the government aspires to reach in the long run.

Package of basic services for the extremely poor

The initiative to extend the health care coverage to the extremely poor segment of the population through the delivery of a basic health package benefited some 6 million people by 1997. The significance of this measure is that it is a crucial step towards ensuring universal access to a set of basic health care services for the entire population in the long run. Although designed primarily for those living in remote rural areas, it is the first time such a social minimum has been given a concrete definition, without which any policy debate on access issues is bound to remain vague. How comprehensive the package should ultimately be is largely a political choice, determined according to affordability and trade-offs with other priority expenditures. But a clear definition of what constitutes a minimum set of health care services to which every citizen is entitled should be a cornerstone in any future system ensuring universal coverage.

Reform of the IMSS financing and membership rules

The financing reform of the IMSS envisages that over the next ten years its revenues will come mostly from a lump-sum payroll tax and general tax revenue of the government. By reducing non-wage labour costs, such a move can be expected to induce more informal sector workers to be registered with the IMSS. The number of people covered under the IMSS health system will likely be boosted further through the new options for voluntary affiliation and the new health insurance scheme for the family. There are uncertainties about both the likely number of new entrants to the system and their medical risks. Experience from other OECD countries suggests that a subsidised, open-ended programme of this kind is likely to experience a large increase in demand. While it may be effective in extending health insurance to the near poor and the middle classes, such a system carries a high financial risk. The voluntary nature of the new options may result in opportunistic behaviour, attracting people only when they experience or expect serious illness. How the various changes in financing and membership rules will affect the future balance of IMSS revenues and expenditures is difficult to predict, though experience in other countries (as well as the nature of health insurance and demand for health care services) suggests that demand for health care will substantially outstrip resources made available. The reform proposals are silent on rationing procedures envisaged should excess demand develop. In such circumstances it is likely that there will be increased queuing – which is a highly inefficient way of rationing.

The "opting-out" facility

The possibility of opting-out to receive services from managed care organisations is seen by the government as a way of enhancing the IMSS's ability to deal with increased demand resulting from coverage expansion: This is to come about by releasing extra capacity which would otherwise be used by those choosing this option, and through improved efficiency in IMSS health care provision due to increased competitive pressure. Experience in other countries suggests, however, that those who opt out tend to have lower medical risks than the average – known as the problem of adverse selection – a likelihood which is heightened by the expansion of IMSS coverage and new voluntary affiliation programmes. It is questionable whether the set of associated regulations, which is part of the reform plan, will be sufficient to eliminate the adverse selection problem. If the latter persists, the demand for IMSS services will not be reduced as much as expected under the opting-out facility, implying an increased fiscal risk as the IMSS is increasingly financed through the government's general revenues. Moreover, the competitive effects on IMSS are likely to materialise only if the IMSS is willing to forego the in-house provision of health care services and rely instead on purchasing these services from providers operating in contestable markets. While this is indeed envisaged in the long-term government reform plans, the transition will take time. The IMSS intends to proceed through open consultation in which all interested parties are to express their position. It also views gradualism in the implementation of changes as a key element for the success of the reform.

The opting-out facility could even run counter to achieving the long-term reform objective of creating a system organised by key functions, if it amounts to setting up other parallel sub-systems based on employment relations, as is currently the case with PEMEX and ISSSTE. For the option to be consistent with the long-term reform of the Mexican health system, it is necessary to separate the functions of purchasing health services (the role of the health insurance) and the provision of such services by independent enterprises (*e.g.* hospitals and practitioners) which compete in contestable markets, subject to some quality supervision by the SSA. A pertinent regulatory framework will need to be established – requiring that a well-defined set of services be provided and not allowing refusals – so as to avoid "cream skimming" and segmenting the risk pool. Setting up private health insurance schemes based on employment relations, as implied by the opting-out facility, can also act as an impediment to labour mobility and/or cause problems for persons losing their job, as experience in the United States shows.

Decentralisation of IMSS and SSA

Coverage expansion and the underlying growth in demand for services are likely to strain the system of public health service provision which has already been suffering from poor quality and inefficiency. The government's reform plan envisages improvements in quality and efficiency through decentralisation of IMSS and SSA health services. While benefits of decentralisation are potentially high in Mexico, the experience in other Latin American countries suggests that poorly implemented decentralisation can worsen rather than solve problems – at least in the short run. In order to maximise the probability of success, decentralisation should be phased in gradually, taking into account differences in management and administrative capabilities at lower levels of government and regional IMSS offices. Current extensive preparations under way to push the decentralisation process further suggest that the authorities are aware of these risks, and, in combination with experience from past decentralisation efforts, this should increase chances that these reforms – which seem anyway inevitable in the long run – will be implemented efficiently. It may be worth investigating whether there are any synergies to be gained by combining the decentralisation reforms with efforts to separate the purchaser and provider functions in both the SSA and IMSS.

Reducing inequity in resource allocation among states

In parallel with decentralisation, efforts have been made to correct the large imbalances in allocation of SSA funds among different states through an improved formula which takes into account different demographic and epidemiological features across regions. This is not only consistent with the government's proclaimed equity objectives, but will also facilitate the eventual introduction of risk-adjusted capitation payments for delivery of essential health care services, a payment method which is widely considered to be more conducive to cost containment than fee-for-service arrangements. The principles underlying the funding allocation formulas of IMSS and SSA are very similar and should also be adopted by other social security institutions.

What remains to be done

Current reform measures are bringing about a significant expansion of health care coverage. While some efficiency gains can be expected from decentralisation and on-going technical improvements, these are unlikely to be large enough to cope with the coverage expansion as well as the underlying growth in demand for health care. Pending a more radical institutional reform, there is likely to be a significant increase in health spending in the medium term. Yet a radical reform to dismantle walls between parallel vertically integrated systems and to re-organise contracting arrangements for payment and service provision takes time, and the list of required future actions is long. Priority should therefore be placed on those actions which are of particular strategic importance in ensuring an efficient transition to the new system.

At the level of general practitioners, both in the IMSS primary care services and in public institutions in urban areas where the number of doctors is sufficient, an important measure should be to give patients free choice of the general practitioner (family doctor), and introduce a capitation component in doctors' earnings, to create an incentive for them to improve the quality of services so as to attract and keep patients. Also general practitioners' role as gatekeepers needs to be reinforced to improve patients' referral system to specialist doctors, which is often inadequate; however, a proper incentive mechanism for general practitioners is required, as shown by the United Kingdom experience, to reduce the risk of "competitive" (*i.e.* excessive) referral. Third, the authorities should proceed, as planned, with the introduction of incentive payments, through bonuses, for instance, for general practitioners in rural areas, to reduce the regional imbalances in physician/patient ratios.

Important for the transition concerning hospitals are measures which help to raise both the autonomy of public hospitals (both SSA and IMSS) and their budgetary transparency. The introduction of prospective funding methods, which have proven to be effective elsewhere in improving hospital efficiency, would be an example of such measures.[79] The resulting efficiency gains are desirable in any event, and the improved management and cost information about the provision of hospital services will be necessary to enable these hospitals to eventually operate under contracts with insurers, both private and public. Instituting such a system would constitute a crucial first step towards splitting the dual functions of SSA and IMSS as purchaser and provider of health care services, a change which is a crucial element in the government's long-term strategy.

As public hospitals are made autonomous there will have to be an appropriate regulatory and supervisory framework for these bodies, a task earmarked for the SSA in the long-term reform strategy. Even if complete autonomy is not granted to public hospitals, there is a strong need for having such a framework for private medical service providers. As public and private service providers are expected to compete in the future, such a framework should provide a level-playing field.

Summing up, the Mexican government has embarked on an ambitious, wide-ranging reform of the health care system. The large uncertainties about how various design principles are going to be translated into new organisational structures suggests that it is important to analyse and monitor carefully the longer-term systemic implications of any new reform measures. It also points to the usefulness of experimentation using pilot projects, possibly in the form of differentiated speed of implementation of reforms across regions and states. While such a step-by-step approach will clearly facilitate necessary institution-building and thus an orderly transition from the old to the new system, it is to be hoped that it would also make it easier to deal with the political resistance to many of the key reform proposals, that is likely to emanate from powerful vested interests.

Notes

1. Developments reviewed in the following paragraphs refer to national accounts data at constant 1993 prices; quarterly series have been seasonally adjusted by the OECD Secretariat. The turnaround in activity occurred in the middle of 1995, and growth picked up significantly as from the start of 1996. Because of the mobile Easter holiday, the number of working days in the first and second quarters can vary from one year to the next. To avoid this factor from distorting reported 1996-97 developments, the discussion below will focus on changes from one half year to the next (at annual rates), rather than on quarterly developments.

2. In the early 1980s, manufactured good exports made up only 20 per cent of total exports. Total exports of goods and services, in turn, rose with the opening of the economy, to 20 per cent of nominal GDP in 1994, and to 30 per cent in 1997, reflecting the 1995-96 export boom.

3. In 1996, spending by the broad public sector accounted for 60 per cent of the construction sector's total output, while 9 per cent of output pertained to projects built by the private sector under concession schemes; the remaining 31 per cent corresponded to private construction projects in the formal sector of the construction industry. Excluding construction of physical infrastructure, real output in the construction sector (including residential and non-residential building) continued to fall throughout 1996.

4. The protracted slump in retail sales until the middle of 1997 (mainly linked to final consumption of goods), contrasts with developments in wholesale trading, which fell less in 1995 and picked up from the start of 1996. This divergence reflects two factors: first, wholesale trading is more broadly determined by productive activities, including exporting industries, than retail sales; second it covers activities in the informal sector which expanded relatively in the aftermath of the crisis.

5. Household spending on non-durables, although spread widely across income categories, represents as much as 62 per cent of total spending for low-income households. In the case of durable goods, three-quarters of expenditure are made by the 20 per cent of households in the higher-income categories, (cf. INEGI Household Survey of Income and Expenditure, 1994)

6. For a detailed discussion of the Mexican labour market and the significance of alternative unemployment measures, see the 1996 OECD *Economic Survey* on Mexico, Part III.

7. The Agreement for economic recovery (ARE) was signed in October 1995, the Alliance for economic growth (ACE) in October 1996. In the context of the ACE, the prices of gasoline and of diesel fuels increased by 8 per cent in December 1996, followed by monthly increases set at 1.03 and 1.20 per cent respectively – implying a cumulative 12-month increase of about 20 per cent, exceeding the target inflation for December 1997. A schedule for adjustments in

electricity rates is also included. Altogether, prices of goods and services produced by the public sector account for 10.1 per cent of the CPI.

8. Non-*maquiladora* activities, which at present account for more than half of manufacturing exports, are less concentrated on the border area than *maquiladoras,* although they still tend to be located in the north and centre of the country. In January-October 1997, exports by non-*maquiladoras* expanded by 14.3 per cent over the same period a year earlier, while *maquiladoras'* exports increased by 21.7 per cent (in dollar terms).

9. Developments in foreign trade prices and volume refer to OECD Secretariat estimates based on the Bank of Mexico trade data in dollar terms with the price indices for exports and imports elaborated by the Bank being used as deflators.

10. Tourism receipts (US$7 billion in 1996) account for 64 per cent of total receipts on non-factor services, while tourism spending (US$3.4 billion in 1996) represents only one-third of non-factor service expenditure. Net tourism receipts have been rising steadily since the onset of the crisis, reflecting both a slowdown of Mexicans travelling abroad and increased travel by foreigners in Mexico. In the first half of 1997, net tourism receipts increased further, despite the moderate recovery of Mexican tourism abroad.

11. Net interest paid on the public external debt is exposed to changes in international interest rates for the part of the debt contracted at variable rates (one-third of the government's foreign debt). Domestic interest rates also have an impact on interest payments abroad, to the extent that part of the domestic debt is held by non-residents.

12. FDI amounted to US$9.5 billion and 7.6 billion respectively in 1995 and 1996. Over that period, Mexico was, after China, the country that attracted the largest amount of FDI, which reached 2.2 per cent of Mexico's GDP, 14 per cent of gross capital formation, and 18 per cent of private investment.

13. The level of reinvested profits, although a small share of FDI, is its most stable component, reaching between US$1.4 and US$2.4 billion per year in 1993-96. While profits in dollars on FDI contracted by 9 per cent in 1995, the proportion reinvested in Mexico did not decline, as companies with foreign capital – often export-oriented – decided to expand capacity. Of the US$3.9 billion FDI recorded in the balance of payments for the first half of 1997, 1 billion was reinvested profits (equivalent, on an annual basis, to past results).

14. Between 500 000 and 600 000 new residential units need to be built each year to accommodate the increase in the number of households. About half of these are built in the formal sector which has access to banking or other types of credit, the rest corresponds to own-constructions or micro-enterprises. Although the latter type of house building did not suffer as much over the past two years, it will take several years for households' financial situation to recover, hence for the backlog accumulated in 1995-96 to be absorbed.

15. Defined in 1995 by the monetary authorities to correspond to consumer price inflation in the 0-3 per cent range.

16. The daily pre-announced crawling peg was replaced by an intervention band that was made progressively wider; see the OECD 1995 Survey for a detailed review of developments in 1994-95.

17. Demand for base money consists largely of bills and coins held by the non-bank public as banks face a zero reserve requirement, and the banking system's voluntary reserve holdings

are limited to vault cash and are thus very low. Demand for bills and coins follows a stable seasonal pattern that the Bank accommodates elastically.

18. As deposits in the central bank bear no interest, there is an opportunity cost on positive average balances, while overdrafts are charged twice the 28-day Cetes rate.

19. Net international assets increased by US$5.9 billion, substantially more than the minimum US$1.4 billion increase stated in the monetary programme. The Bank's foreign exchange purchases from the private sector (US$909 million) took place in periods of incipient peso appreciation during which holders of options to purchase foreign exchange exercised their rights. The Bank also acquires foreign exchange directly from the public sector; these purchases received a boost in 1996 due to higher-than-expected oil export revenues and the successful placement of international debt issues by the federal government

20. The central bank's econometric estimates point to the significance of real wages as a determinant of demand for base money.

21. As growth prospects were revised upward, the January's monetary programme projection for real output growth is somewhat higher than the assumption used in preparation of the government's November budget document.

22. Net international assets is a broader concept than international reserves. The latter includes only short-term claims and liquid assets, while the former also includes other international assets and liabilities of the central bank. Net international assets have been rising faster than reserves in large part due to the fact that the Bank has repaid some longer-term foreign liabilities, such as IMF loans. Net international reserves amounted to US$22 billion at the end of the first semester of 1997, an increase of some US$4.5 billion since end-1996.

23. Volatility of the nominal exchange rate has been reduced partly because movements in interest rates have taken on a larger role in absorbing shocks, which to some extent may reflect central bank preferences.

24. The most meaningful indicator of the fiscal policy stance would be the change in the cyclically adjusted primary surplus. With potential output data for Mexico not available, this adjustment can not be done. Given the sharp downturn in 1995, the discretionary fiscal tightening would be larger than suggested by the swing in the unadjusted balances, while in 1996, with the recovery, the degree of relaxation would be larger.

25. The public sector accounts discussed in this section follow the same definitions as the information contained in the Ministry of Finance reports to Congress and the Central Bank's Annual Report.

26. Similarly, in 1995, provisions (equivalent to 0.8 per cent of GDP) had been made for the cost of the support measures for small debtors (ADE).

27. Regarding income tax, enterprises can spread losses over 10 years; the carry-over had been overestimated in the budget projections for 1996 and this made up for the shortfall in income tax revenue resulting from the unexpected harshness of the recession. The revenue shortfall from the VAT reflects three main factors: first, the demand composition of the recovery differed from that projected, with less consumption expenditure (subject to VAT) and more exports (VAT-exempt). Second, non-budgeted VAT reduction measures were introduced in January 1996 (zero rate applied to domestic water consumption; only the real interest on consumer debt to be taxed). Finally, there may have been a larger-than-expected degree of tax

evasion and avoidance following the 1995 VAT rate increase. During 1996, an "amnesty" was granted to induce tax payers to pay their debt by granting them a 50 per cent discount on their cumulated tax obligation. Administrative procedures to improve tax collection have also been put in place, and they seem to be yielding some result as evidenced by tax revenue in 1997I.

28. Capital expenditure reached 3.7 per cent of GDP in both 1994 and 1996, compared with 3 per cent of GDP in 1993. Caution is needed when interpreting trends over several years because of the divestiture of public enterprises. By 1993, data concerning the largest public enterprises, such as Telmex, were recorded in the private sector.

29. Privatisation proceedings affected 65 public enterprises in 1996, of which 30 had been initiated that same year; 21 privatisation operations were concluded in 1996. The revenue from divestiture of public enterprises is not included in the public sector financial balance, in accordance with the usual accounting practice in Mexico and international norms. Privatisation of public enterprises and the sale of concessions are reviewed in more detail in Chapter III below.

30. Excluding the cost of the social security reform, the primary surplus was projected to reach 4 per cent of GDP in 1997. Half of the estimated cost on that account reflects increased government contributions to the health insurance scheme, the other half is due to the pension reform (see Chapters III and IV below).

31. These two measures are estimated in the budget to have a potential positive effect on revenue equivalent to $1/2$ per cent of GDP.

32. The "Build-Lease-Transfer" (BLT) operations are not reflected in the 1997 budget accounts. They will be recorded in the financial accounts of the public sector when the projects are completed and delivered; at that time, payment will be scheduled by instalments from budget resources, while the flow of revenues from operating the project will alleviate pressure on the budget.

33. These figures refer to data reported by the Ministry of Finance. According to the Bank of Mexico methodology, the broad net debt of the public sector, including official financial intermediaries (development banks and development trust funds) amounted to 31 per cent of GDP at the end of December 1995 (up 10 percentage points from the level a year earlier). After consolidation with the central bank, *i.e.* excluding net financing from the central bank to the rest of the public sector, the net debt amounted to 29.5 per cent of GDP in 1995 (against 19.9 per cent in December 1994), falling to 26.1 per cent of GDP in 1996.

34. In July 1996, the floating rate notes had been placed with an interest rate of Libor plus 200 basis points, 177 basis point below the rate on the original US loan; they were guaranteed by proceeds from exports of crude oil and oil derivatives. The August 1997 redemption was financed by resources raised through a number of placements of fixed income debt instruments in various currencies. As a basis for comparison, in April 1997, the Federal government was issuing 5-year floating rate securities at Libor plus 125 basis points.

35. In September 1997, Bondes and Udibonos together accounted for 57 per cent of the gross public debt, while the share of Cetes (treasury bills) in the total was 35 per cent.

36. PRONAFIDE notes that new information may lead to revisions of the baseline scenario.

37. As noted above, these inflation figures represent an upper bound rather than official targets. In fact, the entire scenario should be interpreted more as an indicative macro-economic framework to facilitate discussion of medium-term policy priorities than as a list of policy objectives or forecasts.

38. Data from the household income and expenditure survey– though it may be subject to problems of under-reported income – show that household saving is concentrated in the higher income categories (deciles 8 to 10), while the lower income categories (deciles 1 to 4) have negative savings. Additional evidence pointing to low marginal saving over the short term is the current backlog in real private consumption, which in the second quarter of 1997, two years after its 1995 trough, was more than 6 per cent below its pre-crisis level, and even below its 1992 level – implying an even larger cut in per capita consumption.

39. Failure of households to increase their saving in response to higher real rates of return would be indicative of pertinent consumer preferences; it is questionable whether government intervention to correct such an outcome is justifiable on general welfare grounds.

40. In the face of stronger competition banks will have to squeeze operating margins, and this in turn can entice them to seek deposits more actively. Development of a network of small savings institutions (*cajas de ahorros*) is starting, which is thought to facilitate collecting lower-income households savings.

41. The PRONAFIDE seems to imply that by limiting the current balance deficit to 3 per cent of GDP large swings in capital flows are both less likely and easier to handle. It also points out that a substantial increase in the share of FDI in net capital inflows might justify raising this threshold.

42. The review of progress in structural reform presented below does not cover agriculture and regional developments; comprehensive reviews of structural policies in both these areas have just been published by the OECD: *Review of Agricultural Policies in Mexico* (1997) and *Regional Development and Structural Policy in Mexico* (1997).

43. The number of pupils receiving money transfers for school attendance at the lower secondary level – where the population expands rapidly because of demographic dynamics – increased by 12 per cent in the school year 1996-97, from a year earlier. Slightly more money is granted for higher levels of basic education than for lower levels, reflecting the higher opportunity cost of not working for older pupils, and to females than to males because of the potential external effect of female education for family health and nutrition.

44. The number of grants under PROBECAT (Scholarships for Training Programme) increased four-fold to 200 000 between 1993 and 1994. In January 1995, it was announced that the scope of the programme would be expanded to 350 000 grants (instead of the 250 000 originally planned); then in March, in view of the quick deterioration of the labour market, a further expansion was decided. In the event, the number of grants had risen to 500 000 in 1996. The CIMO (Quality and Modernisation programme) measures were also strengthened in 1995 and 1996 to help workers in smaller enterprises (Table 15).

45. The need for considering action in these areas is analysed in some detail in the OECD 1996 *Economic Survey* on Mexico, Chapter III.

46. In the past, contributions to the IMSS pension scheme were used to finance expenditure of the health and maternity component which exceeded contributions earmarked for this purpose. As

a result IMSS would have been unable to meet its pension obligations in the longer run, as contributors moved into retirement.

47. Background information on Mexico's pension system before and after the reform was presented in the 1996 *Economic Survey of Mexico*, Annex II.

48. The worker will be given the choice between contracting a life rent with an insurance company or programming a retirement plan (in the latter case he keeps the option to switch to an annuity contract at any time). Resources raised under the INFONAVIT scheme are combined on retirement with the pension resources to buy the annuity (if the worker did not obtain a housing loan). A new mechanism for paying contributions was established in 1997, whereby all social contributions are integrated. Funds collected by the banks are transferred to the central bank which allocates them respectively to IMSS for health, life and accident insurance, and to the selected AFOREs for the pension component.

49. When the reform of the IMSS health fund (reviewed in Chapter IV) is taken into account, the total cost for the budget is about double that amount, *i.e.* $1\frac{1}{2}$ to 2 per cent annually over the next 20 years or so.

50. Only an update on recent developments in these areas is presented here; for a review of past changes, see the 1995 and 1996 *Economic Surveys* on Mexico.

51. PEMEX gives private companies open access to its pipelines so that they can transport privately distributed gas on equal terms. Whether this will be sufficient to develop competition will depend crucially on what is meant by "equal terms". Only if all users enjoy the same terms of access as PEMEX gives to itself will competition take place on a level playing field.

52. In the case of the first co-generation plant being built by a US-Mexican consortium in the border state of Chihuahua, the CFE will pay a predetermined lease for a period of 20 years, at the end of which the plant becomes its property.

53. Agreement was reached in the Economic Deregulation Council on the elimination and simplification of business formalities applied by the Ministries of Health, Labour, Tourism and Environment, and approximately two-thirds of the proposed changes have been legally implemented. A "fast track" licensing system has been implemented in Mexico City to allow the vast majority of new businesses to open within seven to 21 days.

54. Since January 1997, the whole amount of a loan that is delinquent is recorded as non performing, in line with treatment of non-performing loans under internationally accepted accounting principles. In the past only the portion of the loan that was due and unpaid was recorded as non performing.

55. Deposits and branch offices of five banks (Cremi, Oriente, Union, Obrero, Interestatal) have been transferred to sound banks. Three banks have already been sold as going concerns (Inverlat, Centro and Banpais). Authorities are proceeding with the sale of two other banks (Confia and Sureste). The remaining three banks under official control (Capital, Promotor del Norte, Anahuac) will be liquidated, merged or sold as soon as possible.

56. By June 1995 the amount of loans outstanding had reached some 7 billion pesos. A year later only two banks continued to receive support through PROCAPTE and the balance of loans outstanding had declined to 2.9 billion pesos. In the second half of 1996, one of these banks required additional support and the balance mounted to 11.9 billion pesos. The quick close-

down of the programme is in line with original programme design. The main incentive for share-holders to re-pay the loan on schedule is that if subordinated loans were converted into equity, the shareholders would lose control of the bank.

57. The condition is that new equity capital be brought into the bank at a rate of one peso for two pesos of loans purchased by FOBAPROA. In the case of non-convertible subordinated debentures, new capital must be brought in at the rate of one-for-one.

58. The original UDI (Units of investment) programme is discussed in more detail in the 1996 Mexico Survey. In UDI restructuring, bank loans are restructured into index-linked debts. The government provides funding for the UDI (inflation adjusted) loans at a below market rate that the bank then passes on to the borrower. The scope of these operations has been limited by the availability of UDI funds granted by the government.

59. Cut-off dates for FINAPE are December 1996 and January 1997 for starting restructuring negotiations regarding credits granted before June 1996 and July 1996, respectively.

60. An amount equivalent to 2.2 percentage points of GDP is already reflected in public sector financial accounts and does not need to be financed (either it has been paid for or it is included in the public debt).

61. Premature death is defined here as ''potential years of life lost'' (PYLL), a concept developed by the World Health Organisation (WHO). PYLL is measured as the number of years remaining to age 70 for those who die before that age from all causes except suicide. The measure gives an indication of loss of life which could have been prevented if medical knowledge had been applied, if known public health principles had been in force, and if risky behaviours had not been so prevalent. A fall in the indicator reflects an improvement in health outcome. (*Source:* OECD health database, calculated on the basis of WHO information).

62. Long-term simulations indicate that future pressure on health spending in Mexico will mainly come from chronic and/or degenerative diseases characteristic of ageing populations, although the age structure of the population implies that this pressure will peak later than for most other OECD countries (CONAPO, 1995).

63. The discussion of problems in the Mexican health care system before the reform is based on information provided by national authorities (Ministry of Health, in particular) as well as IMSS (1996), FUNSALUD, (1994, 1996, 1997).

64. Recognising the destitute conditions of health care facilities in several regions, due to lack of infrastructure maintenance or absence of personnel, the World Bank financed a project for the support of Health Services to the non-insured population from the four poorest states in 1991-95; the programme has been extended to the period 1996-2000 covering several hundred municipalities in eighteen states.

65. This pattern likely reflects lower demand for SSA services relative to capacity because of poorer quality, as expressed in users' surveys.

66. Health experts of the Mexican institution FUNSALUD use the average of two estimates in their 1997 study, a higher estimate based on national accounts data and a lower one based on the National Survey of Households Income and Expenditure. According to the OECD health database, relying on information provided by national authorities, total spending was the equivalent of 5.3 per cent of GDP in 1994. This section is based on estimates published in FUNSALUD, 1997.

67. Pertinent recommendations were made by the World Bank (1993). Although analysis in this domain is difficult because multiple factors influence health outcomes, there is consensus that health interventions to prevent and cure infectious and parasitic diseases and perinatal health problems (through primary health care and preventive measures) are more cost-effective than treatment of chronic and degenerative diseases, characteristic of more urbanised and ageing populations. For an assessment of the Mexican situation in this regard, see Federal Government (1996).

68. The classification of health care systems presented here refers to that used in OECD, (1994).Under the OECD terminology, the organisational structure of the Mexican health care system would be characterised as a segmented "public integrated model".

69. Out-of-pocket spending on private care by individuals who are covered by a social security scheme are an indication of patients' dissatisfaction with the quality of services offered by the public health system.

70. Mexico has one doctor per 652 inhabitants, a ratio comparable to those in other middle income countries; but there is only one nurse per 495 inhabitants, half the proportion observed in comparable countries; the physician/nurse ratio in 1994 was 1: 1.5 instead of a recommended 1: 2 (World Bank, 1993). Although the number of doctors is adequate in the aggregate, doctors tend to be concentrated in urban areas, while rural posts remain unfilled because of poor living conditions (combined with the absence of incentives and inadequate supervision).

71. In the SSA and the IMSS, patients should not enter a general hospital without referral from a primary physician (except in case of emergency or in rural areas where patients are allowed to go the nearest hospital even if it is of secondary level); a referral is also necessary for visits to specialists or analyses. But the population often finds ways to circumvent the rules. The emergency route is often used to enter hospitals, which reduces the institutions' ability to plan and to treat patients at the most cost-effective level.

72. Stiglitz (1988) analyses problems generally associated with private provision of health care; for more details on the Mexican case, see Frenk and Londoño (1997).

73. IMSS registers show that in 1993 one out of five workers were contributing to IMSS on the basis of earnings of one minimum wage or less, while in the national Employment Survey, only one out of forty workers were earning such low wages (IMSS, 1996).

74. Investment expenditures and staff salary increases will continue to be decided at the centre.

75. The majority of the banking sector has been operating under such a scheme, providing private health insurance for its staff, and being partially reimbursed for compulsory IMSS contributions (without risk adjustment). The separate health care systems run by state owned PEMEX and by ISSSTE for their respective staff can also be interpreted as variants (albeit rather different ones) of opting out from IMSS health insurance. In all these cases the arrangements were made to accommodate existing sectoral health insurance schemes when the "comprehensive" IMSS was founded in the 1940s.

76. For an assessment of the first decentralisation, as well as examples of interesting innovations introduced by some states, cf. Cardoso Brum (1993, 1996).

77. The new formula applies to the additional budget once the states have received resources necessary to maintain a similar capacity of response as in the previous year (in real terms).

78. Resources started to be decentralised in 1996 for the purchase of medicine (although states can consolidate their purchases through a central purchasing unit); for equipment, they were decentralised in 1997; the decentralisation of resources for personal services (subject to centrally determined wage rates) is planned in the future.

79. Under traditional budgeting based on past expenditures hospital managers have incentives to spend all of their budget allocations by the end of the financial year. Under prospective funding methods, on the other hand, budgets are allocated on the basis of expected outputs and their standard costs. Those hospitals which operated more efficiently can keep surpluses, while the less efficient ones will have less money available in the following year. Thus, funds flow from high-cost hospitals to low-cost hospitals, and hospital managers face incentives to raise productivity. See OECD, (1995) for a concrete application of prospective funding methods in the State of Victoria in Australia.

Bibliography

Cardoso Brum, Myriam (1993), "La descentralizacíon de servicios de salud en México", *Gestión y política pública*, Vol. 2, No. 2, Mexico, July-December.

Cardoso Brum, Myriam (1996), "La salud y la reformulacion de la politica para su descentralizacion", Paper presented at the *III Seminario de politica social observatorio social*, Mexico, October.

CONAPO (1995), *The Demand for Health Care in Mexico – An Econometric Analysis*, Mexico, September.

Consejo Nacional de Salud (1995), by Dr Mercedes Juan, Mexico, January.

Federal government (1995), *Plan Nacional de Desarrollo 1995-2000*, Mexico.

Federal government (1996), *Programa de Reforma del Sector Salud, 1995*, Mexico.

Federal Government (1997), *Informe de Ejecucion, 1996*.

Frenk, Julio and Juan-Luis Londoño (1997), "Structured pluralism: towards an innovative model for health system reform in Latin America", in FUNSALUD (1997).

FUNSALUD (1994), *Economía y salud, Propuestas para el avance del sistema de salud en México, Informe final*, Mexico.

FUNSALUD (1996), *Health and The Economy, Overview*, Mexico.

FUNSALUD (1997), *Observatorio de la Salud*, Julio Frenk, ed., Mexico, April.

IMSS (1996), Aportaciones al debate, la Seguridad Social ante el futuro (G. Martinez, ed.).

INEGI (1994), *Encuesta Nacional de Ingreso-Gasto de los Hogares* (ENIGH), Mexico.

Inter-American Development Bank (IDB) (1996), *Annual Report*, Washington D.C.

OECD (1994), *The Reform of Health Care Systems – A Review of Seventeen OECD Countries*, Health Policy Studies No. 5, Paris.

OECD (1995), *Economic Survey: Australia*, Paris.

SSA (1994), *Encuesta Nacional de Salud II*, Mexico.

SSA (1996a), *Boletin de informacion estadistica – Recursos y servicios;* Vol. 1, No. 15, *Daños a la salud*, Vol. 2, No 15, Mexico, September.

SSA (1996b), *Informe de labores 1995-1996*, Mexico, September.

Stiglitz, Joseph E. (1988), *Economics of the public sector*, Second Edition.

World Bank (1993), *World Development Report 1993*, Washington, D.C., July.

World Bank (1997), *World Development Report 1997*, Washington, D.C., July.

Annex

Calendar of main economic events

1996

September

A regulatory framework for railroad services is established to prepare the ground for private participation in public services that are being opened to competition. 16 geographic zones are defined prior to the auctioning of regional concessions in the distribution of natural gas.

October

The Federal Government, the Bank of Mexico and representatives of labour and business sign the social pact for 1997 (Alliance for Economic growth).

December

A regulatory framework for the supply of international long-distance telephone services is established; and regulations for public telephones are issued.

1997

January

The Mexican government repays ahead of schedule the final instalment (US$3.5 billion) of its outstanding debt to the US government under the international financial rescue package. The central bank pays back US$1.5 billion to the IMF, reducing Mexico's outstanding debt to the IMF to US$11.5 billion.

The central bank's monetary programme for the year 1997 is released.

February

The foreign exchange commission puts in place a mechanism whereby the central bank is committed to sell by auction a pre-announced amount of foreign exchange (US$200 million) whenever the Peso market rate on a given day declines by 2 per cent or more from the previous day.

March

Prices and tariffs for regulated activities in the natural gas sector are announced.

The US "certifies" Mexico as an ally in the struggle against drug trafficking despite previous opposition from the US Congress related to the arrest in February of Mexico's top drug official for links with the drugs trade.

April

The Commission for retirement funds (CONSAR) establishes the regulations for the operation of the private administrators of pension funds (AFOREs).

June

The government presents its National Programme for Financing Development (PRONAFIDE).

The guerrilla group ERP which had emerged a year earlier in the state of Guerrero declares a unilateral cease fire to allow the July parliamentary elections to proceed peacefully.

Death of the veteran union leader Fidel Velazquez, Secretary General of the Confederation of Mexican Workers (CTM) for more than 50 years.

A regulatory framework for satellite communications is established: the Federal Commission for Telecommunications is entitled to set specific requirements regarding tariffs, service quality and information from operators and service providers which have significant market power.

July

Mid-term elections for the 500 new members of the Chamber of Deputies and 64 new senators. For the first time ever, the mayor of the Federal District of Mexico City is elected. The ruling party (PRI) loses its absolute majority in the Chamber of Deputies, although it remains the largest political party and retains its absolute majority at the Senate. It also has the majority of governorships across states. The opposition party, PRD, becomes the second largest fraction in the lower house of Parliament; and the PRD's candidate is elected mayor of Mexico City. The PAN holds the third place in the

Chamber of Deputies. It wins another two state governorships – which brings its total to six. Altogether it remains the second party in the number of governors and senators.

August

The government's programme for Education, Health and Nutrition (PROGRESA) to assist people living in extreme poverty is announced. Initially the coverage is restricted to 400 000 households to be reached by the end of the year. Subsequently, the scope of the programme will be increased to benefit more households from more regions.

September

Pension contributions start to be paid into individual pension accounts (managed by the AFOREs).

October

Following the financial market turbulence in Asia, conditions are met for the central bank to make use for the first time of the mechanism of foreign exchange auctions to sell dollars to banks.

November

The Federal Budget proposal for 1998 is submitted to Congress. The preliminary projections proposed by the government are a public sector budget deficit equivalent to 1.25 per cent of GDP, with inflation to be between 12 and 12.5 per cent by year end and GDP growth of 5.2 per cent.

The development bank Nafin and Banamex sign an agreement aimed at facilitating lending to micro, small and medium-sized companies. Nafin will share 50 per cent of the risk involved in loans (of up to 6 million pesos) granted by Banamex to companies with annual sales up to 50 million pesos. With this agreement, three banks (Banamex, Banorte and Bital) have now an automatic credit guarantee from Nafin.

The Lower House of Parliament sets up a subcommittee to review bank bailout programmes and in particular FOBAPROA's expenditures in this context.

Business and labour representatives call for an end of the agreements (so-called "social pacts") which they have periodically negotiated with the government since 1987. The Finance Minister announces that the current model of economic pacts will undergo modifications, and that the social pact agreed upon a year ago stays in force until the end of 1997.

STATISTICAL ANNEX AND STRUCTURAL INDICATORS

Table A. Selected background statistics

	Average 1986-96[1]	1980 price basis				1993 price basis							
		1986	1987	1988	1989	1989	1990	1991	1992	1993	1994	1995	1996
A. Percentage changes from previous year													
Private consumption, volume	1.9	-2.8	-0.1	1.8	6.8	7.3	6.4	4.7	4.7	1.5	4.6	-9.5	2.3
Gross fixed capital formation, volume	2.7	-11.8	-0.1	5.8	6.4	5.8	13.1	11.0	10.8	-2.5	8.4	-29.0	17.7
Public sector	-0.6	-14.2	-12.3	-4.2	3.6	7.1	11.2	0.6	-3.3	0.4	2.9	-19.7	24.7
Private sector	4.2	-10.4	6.4	10.2	7.5	5.3	13.8	14.5	15.0	-3.2	9.8	-31.2	15.8
GDP, volume	2.0	-3.8	1.9	1.2	3.3	4.2	5.1	4.2	3.6	2.0	4.4	-6.2	5.1
GDP price deflator	44.8	73.6	139.7	99.5	25.8	26.5	28.1	23.3	14.4	9.5	8.3	37.9	31.7
Industrial production	2.6	-5.6	2.8	2.8	5.5	6.1	6.7	3.4	4.4	0.3	4.8	-7.8	10.4
Employment[2]	3.6	::	::	4.7	3.6	3.6	1.9	5.5	4.6	4.1	0.9	1.9	5.0
Compensation of employees	46.6	66.4	129.3	97.0	27.7	30.8	34.6	34.3	26.3	18.0	15.0	13.8	::
Productivity (GDP/employment)[3]	0.1	::	::	-3.3	-0.2	1.3	0.2	1.2	2.0	0.8	1.8	-3.4	::
Unit labour cost (compensation/GDP)	44.4	72.9	125.1	94.6	23.6	25.5	28.1	28.9	21.8	15.7	10.1	21.3	::
B. Percentage ratios													
Gross fixed capital formation as % of GDP at current prices	18.3	19.5	18.5	19.3	18.2	17.2	17.9	18.7	19.6	18.6	19.4	16.1	17.2
Stockbuilding as % of GDP at current prices	2.9	-0.9	0.8	1.2	3.2	5.7	5.3	4.7	3.7	2.4	2.4	3.4	3.7
Foreign balance as % of GDP at current prices	-0.1	3.9	6.1	1.5	-0.2	-0.1	-1.1	-2.9	-5.0	-3.9	-4.9	2.9	2.5
Compensation of employees as % of GDP at current prices	30.5	28.5	26.8	26.2	25.7	29.5	29.5	30.9	32.9	34.7	35.3	31.1	::
Unemployment as % of labour force[2]	3.8	4.3	3.9	3.5	2.9	2.9	2.7	2.7	2.8	3.4	3.6	6.3	5.5
C. Other indicator													
Current balance (US$ billion)	-9.9	-1.4	4.2	-2.4	-5.8	-5.8	-7.5	-14.6	-24.4	-23.4	-29.7	-1.6	-1.9

1. The 1980 price basis is used for sub-period 1986-88; the 1993 price basis from then on.
2. National Survey of Urban Employment.
3. National Survey of Employment.
Source: OECD.

Table B. **Gross domestic product and expenditure**

Million pesos, constant 1993 prices

	1986	1987	1988	1989	1990	1991	1992	1993	1994	1995	1996
Private consumption	701 209	702 400	711 453	763 270	812 336	850 343	890 130	903 174	945 070	855 260	875 131
Public consumption	122 440	120 494	119 318	121 939	126 005	132 842	135 312	138 565	142 517	140 643	145 826
Gross fixed capital formation	153 009	153 608	162 548	171 896	194 456	215 833	239 227	233 179	252 745	179 438	211 234
Public	48 815	42 600	40 632	43 526	48 405	48 676	47 071	47 264	48 636	39 031	48 688
Private	104 194	111 008	121 916	128 371	146 051	167 157	192 156	185 916	204 109	140 407	162 545
Stockbuilding	-5 533	4 708	25 874	19 493	19 041	18 895	26 755	30 597	37 245	9 554	29 782
Total domestic demand	971 125	981 211	1 019 193	1 076 599	1 151 838	1 217 913	1 291 424	1 305 515	1 377 578	1 184 894	1 261 974
Exports of goods and services	124 677	136 509	144 376	152 550	160 643	168 788	177 201	191 540	224 953	299 162	355 132
Imports of goods and services	84 524	88 874	121 503	143 334	171 634	197 684	236 462	240 859	290 330	253 131	323 488
Foreign balance	40 153	47 636	22 873	9 216	-10 991	-28 896	-59 261	-49 319	-65 377	46 031	31 644
Gross domestic product	1 011 278	1 028 847	1 042 066	1 085 815	1 140 848	1 189 017	1 232 162	1 256 196	1 312 201	1 230 925	1 293 618

Source: INEGI and OECD.

135

Table C. Gross domestic product and expenditure

Million pesos, current prices

	1980 price basis			1993 price basis								
	1986	1987	1988	1988	1989	1990	1991	1992	1993	1994	1995	1996
Private consumption	54 209	127 268	270 998	281 569	377 907	514 117	669 159	808 120	903 174	1 016 495	1 231 679	1 691 243
Public consumption	7 208	16 995	33 741	35 028	45 383	61 949	86 163	111 752	138 565	164 161	191 981	258 165
Gross fixed capital formation	15 415	35 667	75 199	77 110	94 670	132 113	177 044	220 545	233 179	274 861	296 708	438 039
Public	5 176	10 071	19 717	18 318	23 068	31 585	38 539	42 597	47 264	53 349	60 967	94 461
Private	10 239	25 596	55 482	58 792	71 602	100 528	138 505	177 949	185 916	221 512	235 741	343 578
Stockbuilding	-734	1 566	4 501	16 812	31 254	38 879	44 379	41 563	30 597	33 824	63 247	94 166
Total domestic demand	76 098	181 496	384 439	410 518	549 214	747 059	976 745	1 181 981	1 305 515	1 489 342	1 783 616	2 481 613
Exports of goods and services	13 732	37 692	65 568	82 961	104 266	137 441	155 327	171 476	191 540	236 443	567 322	801 454
Imports of goods and services	10 639	25 877	59 555	77 174	104 622	145 603	182 924	228 123	240 859	305 625	513 162	738 849
Foreign balance	3 094	11 816	6 012	5 787	-356	-8 162	-27 597	-56 646	-49 319	-69 183	54 160	62 605
Gross domestic product	79 191	193 312	390 451	416 305	548 858	738 898	949 148	1 125 334	1 256 196	1 420 159	1 837 776	2 544 219

Source: OECD.

Table D. Gross domestic product by industry of origin

Million pesos, constant prices of 1993

	1986	1987	1988	1989	1990	1991	1992	1993	1994	1995	1996
Agriculture, forestry and fishing	67 340	68 317	65 980	65 892	69 604	71 222	70 533	72 703	73 373	74 099	74 959
Mining and quarrying	14 384	15 099	15 134	15 090	15 602	15 765	15 963	16 258	16 670	16 223	17 575
Manufacturing	168 068	172 365	178 416	192 501	205 525	212 578	221 427	219 934	228 892	217 839	241 487
Construction	42 236	43 416	43 240	43 995	48 040	50 385	53 754	55 379	60 048	45 958	51 197
Electricity, gas and water	14 651	15 199	16 114	16 835	17 270	17 337	17 869	18 327	19 201	19 614	20 492
Wholesale and retail trade, hotels and restaurants	197 649	199 347	202 530	211 892	225 058	238 750	251 402	251 629	268 696	226 896	236 187
Transportation, storage and communication	83 273	85 671	87 505	91 603	94 873	98 125	103 317	107 480	116 842	111 081	120 768
Financial services, insurance and real estate	139 803	144 730	146 785	151 916	158 670	166 125	173 740	183 208	193 146	192 526	195 310
Community services	225 419	225 312	226 562	233 484	240 835	251 629	255 443	263 922	267 243	261 067	263 675
Imputed bank service charge	22 904	23 384	24 039	24 750	26 414	28 559	30 416	33 707	37 436	33 416	32 114
GDP at basic prices	929 919	946 073	958 230	998 459	1 049 064	1 093 358	1 133 032	1 155 132	1 206 674	1 131 889	1 189 537
Taxes on products less subsidies	81 360	82 773	83 837	87 356	91 784	95 659	99 130	101 064	105 526	99 036	104 080
Gross domestic product	1 011 278	1 028 846	1 042 066	1 085 815	1 140 848	1 189 017	1 232 162	1 256 196	1 312 200	1 230 925	1 293 618

Source: OECD.

137

Table E. Cost components of GDP

	1980 price basis			1993 price basis							
	1986	1987	1988	1988	1989	1990	1991	1992	1993	1994	1995
Million pesos											
Compensation of employees	22 605	51 878	102 179	123 951	162 130	218 203	293 064	370 021	436 483	501 897	571 354
Net operating surplus	39 396	97 421	205 898	209 268	284 011	386 459	485 016	551 640	597 279	667 538	889 692
Consumption of fixed capital	10 871	25 284	46 763	47 700	55 120	68 039	84 911	100 204	113 388	129 563	210 842
Indirect taxes	8 541	23 523	42 548	42 323	56 052	74 857	93 900	112 508	119 862	131 036	178 982
less Subsidies	2 222	4 812	6 937	6 937	8 455	8 660	7 743	9 039	10 816	9 875	13 094
Gross domestic product	79 191	193 312	390 451	416 305	548 858	738 898	949 148	1 125 334	1 256 196	1 420 159	1 837 776
Per cent of GDP											
Compensation of employees	28.5	26.8	26.2	29.8	29.5	29.5	30.9	32.9	34.7	35.3	31.1
Net operating surplus	49.7	50.4	52.7	50.3	51.7	52.3	51.1	49.0	47.5	47.0	48.4
Consumption of fixed capital	13.7	13.1	12.0	11.5	10.0	9.2	8.9	8.9	9.0	9.1	11.5
Indirect taxes	10.8	12.2	10.9	10.2	10.2	10.1	9.9	10.0	9.5	9.3	9.7
less Subsidies	2.8	2.5	1.8	1.7	1.5	1.2	0.8	0.8	0.9	0.7	0.7

Source: OECD.

Table F. **Prices and real wages**

	1980 price basis				1993 price basis							
	1986	1987	1988	1989	1989	1990	1991	1992	1993	1994	1995	1996[1]
Real earning by occupied person[2] (1988 = 100)												
Total	111.9	108.6	100.0	105.1	105.9	107.4	114.2	122.8	130.6	136.9	118.8	∷
Agriculture	126.1	117.3	100.0	95.6	97.8	87.6	87.9	86.2	85.1	84.2	72.8	∷
Manufacturing	101.4	100.5	100.0	106.7	108.4	107.9	111.5	117.3	118.7	123.2	106.9	∷
Construction	118.0	113.9	100.0	95.5	94.3	93.0	94.4	97.5	100.1	103.0	86.8	∷
Commerce, hotels et restaurants	119.8	113.0	100.0	103.1	108.2	112.3	119.4	126.1	132.9	136.5	116.3	∷
Federal government	109.5	111.6	100.0	111.5	106.8	112.0	122.9	135.0	150.7	165.1	142.6	∷
Prices (annual % changes)												
Deflators												
Gross domestic product	73.6	139.7	99.5	25.8	26.5	28.1	23.3	14.4	9.5	8.3	37.9	31.7
Private consumption	82.5	135.1	109.1	23.3	25.1	27.8	24.3	15.4	10.1	7.6	33.9	34.2
Exports of goods and services	78.0	150.7	64.5	21.0	18.9	25.2	7.6	5.2	3.3	5.1	80.4	19.0
Imports of goods and services	135.1	131.3	68.3	13.6	14.9	16.2	9.1	4.3	3.7	5.3	92.6	12.7
Terms of trade	-24.3	8.4	-2.3	6.5	3.5	7.7	-1.4	0.9	-0.3	-0.2	-6.3	5.6
Producer prices	79.5	145.3	99.3	12.8	12.8	22.7	19.1	12.0	6.6	6.4	41.5	34.3
Consumer prices[3]	105.7	159.1	51.7	19.7	19.7	29.9	18.8	11.9	8.0	7.1	52.0	27.7
Basic basket[4]	125.3	155.9	41.6	15.4	15.4	33.6	22.3	8.1	7.5	8.1	60.6	33.3
Other goods and services	94.8	161.3	58.0	22.1	22.1	27.9	16.8	14.1	8.3	6.5	46.6	24.4

1. Provisional.
2. Deflated by the consumer price index.
3. December to December.
4. Basic goods and services, of which some supplied by the public sector (gasoline, electricity).
Source: Banco de México; INEGI and OECD.

Table G. **Federal government revenue and expenditure**

Billion pesos

	1986	1987	1988	1989	1990	1991	1992	1993	1994	1995	1996[1]
Total revenue	12.7	33.0	68.0	90.2	117.7	147.5	180.3	194.8	215.3	280.1	392.9
Tax revenue	11.9	30.9	60.8	78.9	105.2	134.7	161.0	178.0	191.9	243.6	340.4
Direct taxes	6.3	17.8	32.9	43.9	59.1	75.4	92.4	104.3	104.7	147.2	212.1
PEMEX	3.0	10.2	13.5	18.0	26.1	31.2	34.5	35.0	31.8	73.5	114.6
Income tax	3.4	7.7	19.5	25.9	33.0	44.2	57.9	69.2	72.9	73.7	97.5
Indirect taxes	5.6	13.1	27.8	35.0	46.1	59.3	68.6	73.8	87.2	96.4	128.3
VAT	2.5	6.3	14.0	17.0	26.6	32.5	30.5	33.1	38.5	51.8	72.1
Excise taxes	2.2	4.9	10.9	12.6	11.2	11.5	18.2	19.3	27.9	24.7	29.5
Gasoline	1.5	3.3	7.3	8.0	5.2	7.0	12.7	13.4	21.8	17.3	20.3
Other	0.7	1.6	3.6	4.6	6.0	4.5	5.5	5.9	6.1	7.4	9.2
Import duties	0.6	1.5	1.7	3.8	6.3	9.7	12.7	12.5	12.6	11.0	15.0
Other taxes	0.2	0.5	1.2	1.6	2.0	5.5	7.3	8.8	8.2	8.9	11.7
Non-tax revenue	0.8	2.1	7.3	11.3	12.5	12.7	19.3	16.8	23.3	36.5	52.4
Total expenditure	23.0	60.4	105.9	115.8	137.1	147.4	163.9	185.2	221.2	293.1	404.1
Current expenditure	20.5	54.2	98.3	105.9	118.9	126.0	139.0	162.9	188.9	259.1	354.5
Wages, acquisitions, general services and other services	3.1	7.4	13.4	18.5	22.5	33.1	28.3	35.0	42.3	47.9	64.3
Interest	11.2	34.5	60.9	59.8	59.9	43.4	36.5	28.9	27.1	70.3	94.3
Participations and transfers	5.3	11.5	22.2	27.2	34.4	47.7	72.0	96.7	116.4	138.1	191.4
Other[2]	0.9	0.9	1.8	0.4	2.1	1.8	2.2	2.2	3.1	2.8	4.5
Capital expenditure	2.5	6.2	7.5	9.9	18.3	21.5	24.9	22.3	32.3	34.0	49.6
Investment	0.9	1.9	2.2	2.9	5.8	8.4	10.7	12.2	16.8	14.9	23.0
Capital transfers	1.5	4.2	4.9	6.5	11.4	9.2	12.7	8.7	13.5	16.1	24.0
Other[2]	0.1	0.1	0.4	0.5	1.1	3.8	1.4	1.5	2.1	3.0	2.6

1. Preliminary figures.
2. Includes other current transfers, deferred payments and savings.

Source: Ministry of finance.

Table H. Public enterprises under budgetary control: revenue and expenditure[1]

Billion pesos

	1989	1990	1991	1992	1993	1994	1995	1996[2]
A. PEMEX								
Revenues	34.8	51.8	56.6	60.9	64.2	63.0	122.7	188.7
Exports	18.0	24.9	22.5	21.4	19.2	20.0	44.6	73.8
Domestic sales	15.5	25.6	32.7	38.2	43.1	40.1	73.5	108.3
Other	1.3	1.2	1.3	1.3	1.9	3.0	4.6	6.7
Expenditures	36.0	48.7	57.5	63.0	63.5	61.5	119.6	187.1
Operational outlays	13.5	16.5	17.1	18.6	18.3	20.4	29.7	40.6
Interest payments	4.2	5.4	3.7	3.4	3.3	4.4	11.2	13.3
Wages and salaries	2.8	3.4	3.9	4.2	4.2	4.4	4.9	9.6
Other[3]	6.6	7.7	9.5	11.0	10.8	11.5	13.6	17.7
Taxes	18.0	26.3	31.2	34.5	35.0	31.8	73.5	114.6
Capital expenditures	4.4	5.8	8.2	8.7	8.6	10.5	16.0	31.9
Other net flows	0.1	0.1	1.0	1.2	1.5	−1.1	0.4	0.0
Balance on a cash basis	−1.3	3.0	−0.9	−2.1	0.6	1.5	3.1	1.7
B. Other than PEMEX								
Revenues	43.4	55.7	61.1	71.5	83.7	94.5	116.1	146.0
Receipts	22.1	27.0	29.2	32.4	34.4	37.1	41.9	58.2
Transfers	7.8	9.0	7.5	8.2	11.3	12.9	20.1	24.6
Other[4]	13.6	19.4	24.4	30.7	38.0	44.4	54.0	63.3
Capital income	0.0	0.3	0.0	0.2	0.0	0.0	0.0	0.0
Expenditures	42.9	55.8	61.6	69.3	79.9	90.6	107.6	139.5
Operational outlays	35.1	42.9	47.6	56.5	65.1	74.0	90.2	118.2
Interest payments	3.2	1.8	1.2	0.9	1.2	1.4	3.3	2.9
Wages and salaries	9.2	12.6	18.3	22.9	25.8	28.9	33.9	42.4
Other[3]	22.8	28.5	28.1	32.6	38.0	43.7	53.0	72.9
Taxes	0.8	1.6	1.9	2.2	2.5	1.9	3.5	3.1
Capital expenditures	5.8	9.0	10.5	10.7	10.9	14.9	13.7	18.3
Other net flows	1.2	2.3	1.6	−0.2	1.5	−0.2	0.2	0.0
Balance on a cash basis	0.5	−0.1	−0.6	2.2	3.8	3.9	8.5	6.5

1. Including social security and other agencies.
2. Preliminary figures.
3. Includes acquisitions and other expenditures.
4. Includes contributions to social security.

Source: Banco de México.

Table I. **Summary of the financial system**

Million pesos

	1986	1987	1988	1989	1990	1991	1992	1993	1994	1995	1996
Bank of Mexico											
Net international reserves[1]	6 029	28 814	14 551	17 484	29 950	53 886	57 803	76 211	32 739	120 301	137 803
Net domestic credit	- 605	-17 783	2 963	4 740	171	-15 304	-13 831	-29 018	24 196	-53 492	-53 812
Net credit to public sector[2]	3 684	-3 308	9 327	2 951	91	-13 255	-14 673	-19 269	-15 212	-26 200	-16 136
Securities holdings	6 179	13 174	22 138	35 102	39 979	34 668	30 123	9 865	0	13 212	10 488
Credit to financial intermediaries	-4 593	-8 070	-7 887	-5 348	-3 409	4 283	11 987	15 981	70 554	85 136	47 401
Other (net)	-5 875	-19 579	-20 615	-27 965	-36 490	-41 001	-41 268	-35 595	-31 146	-125 640	-95 565
Note issue	3 059	7 318	13 159	17 992	24 603	32 416	38 012	43 228	51 870	60 655	74 091
Banking system											
Net foreign assets	683	1 908	3 136	3 791	5 040	6 571	7 153	7 510	14 602	33 526	45 242
Net domestic credit	61 606	148 188	200 456	272 021	356 912	470 382	573 542	676 358	1 002 443	1 367 379	1 486 462
Net credit to public sector	43 508	92 832	124 070	140 022	145 876	141 378	105 786	65 980	124 465	206 888	194 524
Net credit to private sector	11 464	29 152	53 324	94 872	149 398	233 514	355 592	451 047	643 627	813 396	931 517
Other (net)	6 634	26 204	23 062	37 127	61 639	95 491	112 164	159 331	234 351	347 095	360 421
Medium and long-term foreign obligations	36 090	90 541	90 833	109 714	110 321	124 637	133 685	149 515	292 400	504 451	442 011
Liabilities to nonbank financial intermediaries	4 269	10 705	16 562	21 500	26 743	29 247	32 859	48 862	75 017	131 602	174 195
Liabilities to private sector	24 617	57 836	82 999	119 201	171 682	252 735	317 435	365 753	436 863	592 505	755 394
Monetary aggregates (% of GDP)											
M1	7.3	6.8	5.4	5.7	6.8	11.6	11.2	11.9	10.9	9.0	9.1
M4	38.7	41.0	32.3	36.9	40.1	40.9	41.3	46.8	51.3	47.9	45.8
Interest rate											
3-month Cetes rate	73.93	102.83	58.65	44.77	35.03	19.82	15.89	15.50	14.62	48.24	32.91

1. As defined by the Bank of Mexico Law.
2. Net credit to federal government minus public enterprises deposits.
Source: Banco de México.

Table J. **Balance of payments**

Million dollars

	1986	1987	1988	1989	1990	1991	1992	1993	1994	1995	1996
Current account	**-1 374**	**4 239**	**-2 376**	**-5 821**	**-7 451**	**-14 647**	**-24 438**	**-23 399**	**-29 662**	**-1 577**	**-1 922**
Trade balance[1]	5 020	8 787	2 610	405	-882	-7 279	-15 934	-13 481	-18 464	7 088	6 531
Exports, f.o.b[1]	21 804	27 600	30 691	35 171	40 711	42 688	46 196	51 886	60 882	79 542	96 000
Imports, f.o.b[1]	16 784	18 812	28 082	34 766	41 593	49 967	62 129	65 367	79 346	72 453	89 469
Services, net	-449	334	4	-468	-1 921	-1 751	-2 296	-2 130	-1 968	665	548
Balance on goods and services	4 571	9 121	2 614	-63	-2 803	-9 030	-18 230	-15 611	-20 432	7 753	7 079
Investment income, net	-7 520	-6 801	-7 246	-8 302	-8 626	-8 608	-9 595	-11 429	-13 012	-13 290	-13 532
Transfers, net	1 575	1 919	2 256	2 544	3 979	2 991	3 386	3 640	3 782	3 960	4 531
Capital account	**2 716**	**-1 189**	**-1 163**	**3 669**	**10 292**	**30 839**	**31 202**	**43 199**	**18 668**	**15 925**	**6 318**
Liabilities	2 549	3 609	591	4 839	18 991	31 839	25 650	46 801	24 338	23 283	12 774
Loans and deposits	667	1 978	-3 289	819	10 993	7 992	-1 567	-2 777	1 100	22 952	-11 994
Public sector	2 165	4 035	-1 646	-680	6 577	80	-3 530	-2 209	-361	11 452	-8 918
Bank of Mexico	714	428	-94	1 677	-365	-220	-460	-1 175	-1 203	13 333	-3 524
Commercial banks	-732	47	1 380	980	4 384	5 752	295	3 328	1 471	-4 982	-1 520
Non-financial private sector	-1 481	-2 531	-2 928	-1 157	397	2 381	2 129	2 832	1 193	3 149	1 968
Total foreign investments	1 882	1 631	3 880	4 020	7 998	23 847	27 217	44 025	23 238	331	24 767
Direct investment	2 401	2 635	2 880	3 176	2 633	4 762	4 393	4 389	10 973	9 526	7 619
Portfolio investment	-519	-1 004	1 000	351	3 370	12 753	18 041	28 919	8 182	-9 715	14 154
of which: Stock market	0	0	0	493	1 994	6 332	4 783	10 717	4 084	519	2 995
Assets	167	-4 798	-1 754	-1 170	-8 700	-1 000	5 552	-3 603	-5 670	-7 358	-6 456
In foreign banks	0	-3 885	-74	-177	761	921	2 186	-1 280	-3 714	-3 164	-6 173
Credits to non-residents	-382	-465	-674	-899	-530	19	62	-281	-41	-276	-622
External debt garantees	0	0	-693	-56	-7 354	-604	1 165	-564	-615	-662	544
Other	549	-448	-313	-38	-1 577	-1 335	2 138	-1 477	-1 301	-3 256	-206
Errors and omissions	-739	3 050	-3 195	3 041	2 520	-2 167	-961	-3 142	-3 314	-4 238	373
Changes in reserves (increase = -)	-985	-6 924	7 127	-272	-3 548	-7 378	-1 008	-5 983	18 389	-9 593	-1 768

1. Including maquiladoras trade.
Source: Banco de México.

Table K. Foreign trade by commodity group

Million dollars

	Excluding maquiladoras					Including maquiladoras					
	1987	1988	1989	1990	1991	1991	1992	1993	1994	1995	1996
Total merchandise exports	20 495	20 546	22 842	26 839	26 855	42 688	46 196	51 886	60 882	79 542	96 000
Agriculture, forestry and fishing	1 543	1 670	1 754	2 163	2 373	2 373	2 112	2 504	2 679	4 016	3 592
Mining	576	660	604	617	547	547	356	278	357	545	449
Petroleum	8 630	6 711	7 876	10 104	8 166	8 166	8 307	7 418	7 445	8 422	11 654
Manufactures[1]	9 746	11 504	12 608	13 956	15 769	31 602	35 421	41 685	50 402	66 558	80 305
Food, beverages and tobacco	1 313	1 363	1 268	1 095	1 216	1 421	1 365	1 590	1 896	2 529	2 930
Textiles, clothing and leather	566	619	623	632	764	2 014	2 317	2 770	3 256	4 899	6 339
Chemicals	1 093	1 385	1 537	1 679	1 975	2 120	2 298	2 344	2 756	3 972	4 011
Metal and mineral manufactures	1 707	2 087	2 466	2 409	2 382	2 925	2 993	3 548	3 835	6 293	6 507
Automobiles, motors and parts	3 043	3 414	3 585	4 625	5 383	6 320	7 110	8 671	10 533	14 614	19 193
Machinery and equipment, electronics	1 414	1 823	2 274	2 616	3 090	14 143	16 602	19 682	24 792	30 067	36 543
Other manufactures	610	813	855	900	959	2 659	2 736	3 081	3 334	4 185	4 780
Total merchandise imports	13 305	20 274	25 438	31 272	38 184	49 967	62 129	65 367	79 346	72 453	89 469
Agriculture, forestry and fishing	1 109	1 773	2 003	2 071	2 094	2 131	2 858	2 633	3 371	2 644	4 671
Manufactures	11 941	18 177	23 047	28 812	35 718	47 451	58 751	62 346	75 545	69 209	84 149
Food, beverages and tobacco	460	1 233	2 014	2 679	2 584	2 636	3 336	3 356	3 989	2 616	3 116
Chemicals, petroleum derivatives	2 392	3 050	3 822	4 159	5 139	5 509	6 384	6 825	7 852	7 683	9 452
Metal and mineral manufactures	971	1 659	2 005	2 331	3 189	4 354	5 226	5 099	6 135	5 807	7 214
Metal products, machinery and equipment	6 872	10 248	12 250	15 963	20 132	26 903	33 731	35 673	43 492	39 709	47 462
Other manufactures	1 246	1 987	2 956	3 680	4 674	8 049	10 075	11 393	14 078	13 394	16 905
Other	256	324	388	389	372	385	520	387	430	600	649
Memorandum item:											
In-bond industries (maquiladoras), net	1 598	2 337	3 001	3 551	4 051	4 051	4 743	5 410	5 803	4 924	6 416

1. Not including petrochemicals and petroleum derivatives which are included here in petroleum exports.

Source: INEGI.

Table L. Foreign trade by area[1]

Million dollars

	1986	1987	1988	1989	1990	1991	1992	1993	1994	1995	1996
Exports, f.o.b											
Total	16 158	20 494	20 546	22 842	26 838	42 688	46 196	51 886	60 882	79 542	96 000
OECD countries	14 205	18 126	17 918	20 241	24 205	39 837	42 820	48 187	57 297	73 330	88 137
USA	10 603	13 326	13 534	15 792	18 418	33 912	37 420	43 068	51 855	66 336	80 541
Canada	191	316	278	277	458	1 125	1 000	1 541	1 470	1 979	2 170
Japan	1 057	1 348	1 231	1 314	1 506	1 241	793	700	988	928	1 363
European Union	2 224	3 009	2 727	2 717	3 548	3 339	3 398	2 658	2 748	3 382	3 553
Non-OECD countries	1 953	2 368	2 628	2 601	2 633	2 851	3 376	3 699	3 585	6 212	7 863
Asia[2]	303	410	500	328	324	325	321	436	414	961	1 081
Latin America	1 108	1 437	1 449	1 494	1 514	1 756	2 244	2 597	2 579	4 309	5 166
Imports, f.o.b											
Total	12 433	13 305	20 274	25 438	31 272	49 967	62 129	65 367	79 346	72 453	89 469
OECD countries	10 580	11 428	17 557	21 680	28 545	46 257	57 477	60 283	73 025	67 161	82 847
USA	7 392	7 878	12 607	15 827	20 491	36 814	44 216	46 465	56 913	53 806	67 437
Canada	223	355	338	421	458	670	1 052	1 163	1 600	1 374	1 744
Japan	683	794	1 125	1 081	1 470	1783	3041	3369	3812	3608	3901
European Union	2 025	2 144	2 983	3 669	5 199	6 196	7 651	7 701	8 952	6 724	7 732
Non-OECD countries	1 853	1 877	2 717	3 758	2 727	3 710	4 652	5 084	6 321	5 292	6 622
Asia[2]	155	180	482	760	1 078	1 523	2 199	2 889	3 574	3 686	4 686
Latin America	393	367	730	949	1 595	1 917	2 354	2 471	2 884	1 961	2 240

1. Including maquiladoras as from 1991.
2. Excluding Middle East.
Source: INEGI.

Table M. Production structure and performance indicators [1]

A. Production structure

	Per cent share of GDP at current prices				Per cent share of total employment [2]			
	1980	1985	1990	1995	1980	1985	1990	1995
Agriculture, forestry and fishing	8.2	9.1	7.2	5.0	28.0	27.8	24.0	22.6
Mining	3.2	4.7	2.1	1.6	1.0	1.2	0.7	0.5
Manufactures	22.1	23.4	19.0	19.1	12.0	11.2	12.6	11.3
Food, beverages and tobacco	5.4	6.1	4.5	4.9	3.0	3.0	2.5	2.4
Textiles, clothing	3.0	2.6	1.8	1.5	2.2	1.9	2.0	1.8
Wood and wood products	0.9	0.9	0.7	0.5	0.7	0.6	0.6	0.5
Paper and paper products	1.2	1.3	1.0	1.0	0.6	0.6	0.7	0.6
Chemicals, rubber and plastic products	3.4	4.2	3.5	3.4	1.4	1.5	1.5	1.3
Non-metallic minerals	1.5	1.7	1.4	1.2	0.8	0.8	0.7	0.5
Basic metal products	1.4	1.3	1.3	1.1	0.5	0.5	0.3	0.2
Machinery and equipment	4.8	4.8	4.5	5.2	2.8	2.3	3.8	3.6
Other manufacturing	0.4	0.4	0.3	0.3	0.1	0.1	0.4	0.4
Construction	6.4	4.4	3.6	3.7	9.5	8.9	9.7	9.7
Electricity, gas and water	1.0	0.9	1.2	1.2	0.4	0.5	0.5	0.5
Commerce, restaurants and hotels	28.0	28.1	22.6	19.2	14.5	14.3	17.4	18.9
Transportation and communication	6.4	6.7	8.3	9.1	4.5	4.7	5.5	5.6
Financial services, insurance and real estate	8.6	7.5	12.1	16.8	1.7	2.1	2.0	2.0
Community services	17.2	16.5	16.3	20.7	28.4	29.4	27.5	28.9

B. Manufacturing sector performance

	Productivity growth by sector, real GDP/employment (annual rate)		
	1980/1970	1990/1980	1995/1990
Food, beverages and tobacco	2.4	1.2	2.4
Textiles, clothing	2.8	0.6	0.7
Wood and wood products	2.2	1.7	2.6
Paper and paper products	3.8	2.2	1.7
Chemicals, rubber and plastic products	5.5	1.8	3.2
Non-metallic minerals	4.3	0.5	4.4
Basic metal products	2.2	4.1	13.0
Machinery and equipment	3.6	2.2	1.4

1. Calculated on 1970, 1980 and 1993 price bases respectively.
2. National accounts data, refering to remunerated jobs.
Source: OECD.

Table N. **Labour market indicators**

	A. Labour market performance						
	1986	1991	1992	1993	1994	1995	1996
Unemployment rate[1]							
Total	4.3	2.6	2.8	3.4	3.7	6.2	5.5
Male	3.7	2.5	2.7	3.2	3.6	6.1	5.3
Female	5.3	2.9	3.2	3.9	3.9	6.4	5.9
Dispersion of regional unemployment rates[2]	1.55	1.28	1.14	1.47	1.50	1.65	1.36

	B. Structural and institutional characteristics					
	1960	1970	1980	1990	1995	1996
Participation rate[3]						
Total	46.5	43.6[4]	50.9	51.8	55.4	55.2
Male	78.7	71.7	75.1	71.9	79.3	73.9
Female	15.4	16.4	27.8	33.5	38.0	38.3
Age structure (% of total population)						
0-14	44.2	46.2	43.0	38.3	35.4	
15-24	18.6	18.8	20.7	21.5	21.4	
25-34	13.0	12.1	12.9	14.5	15.6	
35-44	9.4	9.2	9.2	9.9	11.2	
45-64	11.0	9.9	10.1	10.9	11.7	
65 and over	3.7	3.7	4.1	4.8	4.7	

	1960	1970	1990	1991	1993	1995
Employment:[5] share in total						
Primary sector	54.5	41.8	23.4	27.0	27.1	24.7
Secondary sector	19.1	24.4	28.8	23.2	22.2	21.3
Tertiary sector	26.4	33.8	47.8	49.8	50.7	54.0

	Percentage changes (Average annual rates)		
	1970/1960	1990/1970	1995/1988
Employment:[5]			
Total	0.89	3.13	2.69
Primary sector	−1.74	0.19	3.43
Secondary sector	3.39	3.99	−0.49
Terciary sector	3.43	4.92	3.84

1. Unemployed persons, 12 years and over in urban areas. Based on National Survey on Urban Employment.
2. Measured by standard deviation for 16 urban areas (1992, 34 urban areas; 1993, 37 urban areas; 1994 and 1995, 39 urban areas; 1996, 43 urban areas).
3. Labour force as a percentage of relevant population group, aged 12 years and over. Based on National Survey on Urban Employment.
4. Definition not comparable due to change in Census methodology.
5. Based on National Survey of Employment.
Source: INEGI, different surveys and censuses.

BASIC STATISTICS:

INTERNATIONAL COMPARISONS

	Units	Reference period [1]	Australia	Austria
Population				
Total	Thousands	1995	18 054	8 047
Inhabitants per sq. km.	Number	1995	2	96
Net average annual increase over previous 10 years	%	1995	1.4	0.6
Employment				
Total civilian employment (TCE)[2]	Thousands	1994	7 943	3 737
of which: Agriculture	% of TCE	1994	5.1	7.2
Industry	% of TCE	1994	23.5	33.2
Services	% of TCE	1994	71.4	59.6
Gross domestic product (GDP)				
At current prices and current exchange rates	Bill. US$	1995	360.3	233.3
Per capita	US$	1995	19 957	28 997
At current prices using current PPPs[3]	Bill. US$	1995	349.4	167.2
Per capita	US$	1995	19 354	20 773
Average annual volume growth over previous 5 years	%	1995	3.3	2
Gross fixed capital formation (GFCF)	% of GDP	1995	20.1	24.7
of which: Machinery and equipment	% of GDP	1995	10.5 (94)	9 (*)
Residential construction	% of GDP	1995	5.6 (94)	6.4 (*)
Average annual volume growth over previous 5 years	%	1995	3	3
Gross saving ratio[4]	% of GDP	1995	16.9	24.9
General government				
Current expenditure on goods and services	% of GDP	1995	17.2	18.9
Current disbursements[5]	% of GDP	1994	36.2	47.8
Current receipts	% of GDP	1994	34.2	47.3
Net official development assistance	% of GNP	1994	0.33	0.33
Indicators of living standards				
Private consumption per capita using current PPPs[3]	US$	1995	12 090	11 477
Passenger cars, per 1 000 inhabitants	Number	1993	438	418
Telephones, per 1 000 inhabitants	Number	1993	482	451
Television sets, per 1 000 inhabitants	Number	1992	482	480
Doctors, per 1 000 inhabitants	Number	1994	2.2 (91)	2.4
Infant mortality per 1 000 live births	Number	1994	5.9	6.3
Wages and prices (average annual increase over previous 5 years)				
Wages (earnings or rates according to availability)	%	1995	2	5
Consumer prices	%	1995	2.5	3.2
Foreign trade				
Exports of goods, fob*	Mill. US$	1995	53 092	57 200
As % of GDP	%	1995	14.7	24.5
Average annual increase over previous 5 years	%	1995	6	6.9
Imports of goods, cif*	Mill. US$	1995	57 406	65 293
As % of GDP	%	1995	15.9	28
Average annual increase over previous 5 years	%	1995	8.1	5.9
Total official reserves[6]	Mill. SDRs	1995	8 003	12 600
As ratio of average monthly imports of goods	Ratio	1995	1.7	2.3

* At current prices and exchange rates.
1. Unless otherwise stated.
2. According to the definitions used in OECD *Labour Force Statistics*.
3. PPPs = Purchasing Power Parities.
4. Gross saving = Gross national disposable income minus private and government consumption.
5. Current disbursements = Current expenditure on goods and services plus current transfers and payments of property income.
6. Gold included in reserves is valued at 35 SDRs per ounce. End of year.

EMPLOYMENT OPPORTUNITIES

Economics Department, OECD

The Economics Department of the OECD offers challenging and rewarding opportunities to economists interested in applied policy analysis in an international environment. The Department's concerns extend across the entire field of economic policy analysis, both macro-economic and microeconomic. Its main task is to provide, for discussion by committees of senior officials from Member countries, documents and papers dealing with current policy concerns. Within this programme of work, three major responsibilities are:

- to prepare regular surveys of the economies of individual Member countries;
- to issue full twice-yearly reviews of the economic situation and prospects of the OECD countries in the context of world economic trends;
- to analyse specific policy issues in a medium-term context for the OECD as a whole, and to a lesser extent for the non-OECD countries.

The documents prepared for these purposes, together with much of the Department's other economic work, appear in published form in the *OECD Economic Outlook, OECD Economic Surveys, OECD Economic Studies* and the Department's *Working Papers* series.

The Department maintains a world econometric model, INTERLINK, which plays an important role in the preparation of the policy analyses and twice-yearly projections. The availability of extensive cross-country data bases and good computer resources facilitates comparative empirical analysis, much of which is incorporated into the model.

The Department is made up of about 80 professional economists from a variety of backgrounds and Member countries. Most projects are carried out by small teams and last from four to eighteen months. Within the Department, ideas and points of view are widely discussed; there is a lively professional interchange, and all professional staff have the opportunity to contribute actively to the programme of work.

Skills the Economics Department is looking for:

a) Solid competence in using the tools of both microeconomic and macroeconomic theory to answer policy questions. Experience indicates that this normally requires the equivalent of a Ph.D. in economics or substantial relevant professional experience to compensate for a lower degree.

b) Solid knowledge of economic statistics and quantitative methods; this includes how to identify data, estimate structural relationships, apply basic techniques of time series analysis, and test hypotheses. It is essential to be able to interpret results sensibly in an economic policy context.

c) A keen interest in and extensive knowledge of policy issues, economic developments and their political/social contexts.

d) Interest and experience in analysing questions posed by policy-makers and presenting the results to them effectively and judiciously. Thus, work experience in government agencies or policy research institutions is an advantage.

e) The ability to write clearly, effectively, and to the point. The OECD is a bilingual organisation with French and English as the official languages. Candidates must have excellent knowledge of one of these languages, and some knowledge of the other. Knowledge of other languages might also be an advantage for certain posts.

f) For some posts, expertise in a particular area may be important, but a successful candidate is expected to be able to work on a broader range of topics relevant to the work of the Department. Thus, except in rare cases, the Department does not recruit narrow specialists.

g) The Department works on a tight time schedule with strict deadlines. Moreover, much of the work in the Department is carried out in small groups. Thus, the ability to work with other economists from a variety of cultural and professional backgrounds, to supervise junior staff, and to produce work on time is important.

General information

The salary for recruits depends on educational and professional background. Positions carry a basic salary from FF 305 700 or FF 377 208 for Administrators (economists) and from FF 438 348 for Principal Administrators (senior economists). This may be supplemented by expatriation and/or family allowances, depending on nationality, residence and family situation. Initial appointments are for a fixed term of two to three years.

Vacancies are open to candidates from OECD Member countries. The Organisation seeks to maintain an appropriate balance between female and male staff and among nationals from Member countries.

For further information on employment opportunities in the Economics Department, contact:

Administrative Unit
Economics Department
OECD
2, rue André-Pascal
75775 PARIS CEDEX 16
FRANCE

E-Mail: compte.esadmin@oecd.org

Applications citing "ECSUR", together with a detailed *curriculum vitae* in English or French, should be sent to the Head of Personnel at the above address.

MAIN SALES OUTLETS OF OECD PUBLICATIONS
PRINCIPAUX POINTS DE VENTE DES PUBLICATIONS DE L'OCDE

AUSTRALIA – AUSTRALIE
D.A. Information Services
648 Whitehorse Road, P.O.B 163
Mitcham, Victoria 3132   Tel. (03) 9210.7777
                                Fax: (03) 9210.7788

AUSTRIA – AUTRICHE
Gerold & Co.
Graben 31
Wien I   Tel. (0222) 533.50.14
                                Fax: (0222) 512.47.31.29

BELGIUM – BELGIQUE
Jean De Lannoy
Avenue du Roi, Koningslaan 202
B-1060 Bruxelles   Tel. (02) 538.51.69/538.08.41
                                Fax: (02) 538.08.41

CANADA
Renouf Publishing Company Ltd.
5369 Canotek Road
Unit 1
Ottawa, Ont. K1J 9J3   Tel. (613) 745.2665
                                Fax: (613) 745.7660

Stores:
71 1/2 Sparks Street
Ottawa, Ont. K1P 5R1   Tel. (613) 238.8985
                                Fax: (613) 238.6041

12 Adelaide Street West
Toronto, QN M5H 1L6   Tel. (416) 363.3171
                                Fax: (416) 363.5963

Les Éditions La Liberté Inc.
3020 Chemin Sainte-Foy
Sainte-Foy, PQ G1X 3V6   Tel. (418) 658.3763
                                Fax: (418) 658.3763

Federal Publications Inc.
165 University Avenue, Suite 701
Toronto, ON M5H 3B8   Tel. (416) 860.1611
                                Fax: (416) 860.1608

Les Publications Fédérales
1185 Université
Montréal, QC H3B 3A7   Tel. (514) 954.1633
                                Fax: (514) 954.1635

CHINA – CHINE
Book Dept., China National Publications
Import and Export Corporation (CNPIEC)
16 Gongti E. Road, Chaoyang District
Beijing 100020   Tel. (10) 6506-6688 Ext. 8402
                                (10) 6506-3101

CHINESE TAIPEI – TAIPEI CHINOIS
Good Faith Worldwide Int'l. Co. Ltd.
9th Floor, No. 118, Sec. 2
Chung Hsiao E. Road
Taipei   Tel. (02) 391.7396/391.7397
                                Fax: (02) 394.9176

CZECH REPUBLIC –
RÉPUBLIQUE TCHÈQUE
National Information Centre
NIS – prodejna
Konviktská 5
Praha 1 – 113 57   Tel. (02) 24.23.09.07
                                Fax: (02) 24.22.94.33
E-mail: nkposp@dec.niz.cz
Internet: http://www.nis.cz

DENMARK – DANEMARK
Munksgaard Book and Subscription Service
35, Nørre Søgade, P.O. Box 2148
DK-1016 København K   Tel. (33) 12.85.70
                                Fax: (33) 12.93.87

J. H. Schultz Information A/S,
Herstedvang 12,
DK – 2620 Albertslung   Tel. 43 63 23 00
                                Fax: 43 63 19 69
Internet: s-info@inet.uni-c.dk

EGYPT – ÉGYPTE
The Middle East Observer
41 Sherif Street
Cairo   Tel. (2) 392.6919
                                Fax: (2) 360.6804

FINLAND – FINLANDE
Akateeminen Kirjakauppa
Keskuskatu 1, P.O. Box 128
00100 Helsinki

Subscription Services/Agence d'abonnements :
P.O. Box 23
00100 Helsinki   Tel. (358) 9.121.4403
                                Fax: (358) 9.121.4450

*FRANCE
OECD/OCDE
Mail Orders/Commandes par correspondance :
2, rue André-Pascal
75775 Paris Cedex 16   Tel. 33 (0)1.45.24.82.00
                           Fax: 33 (0)1.49.10.42.76
                                Telex: 640048 OCDE
Internet: Compte.PUBSINQ@oecd.org

Orders via Minitel, France only/
Commandes par Minitel, France
exclusivement : 36 15 OCDE

OECD Bookshop/Librairie de l'OCDE :
33, rue Octave-Feuillet
75016 Paris   Tel. 33 (0)1.45.24.81.81
                                33 (0)1.45.24.81.67

Dawson
B.P. 40
91121 Palaiseau Cedex   Tel. 01.89.10.47.00
                                Fax: 01.64.54.83.26

Documentation Française
29, quai Voltaire
75007 Paris   Tel. 01.40.15.70.00

Economica
49, rue Héricart
75015 Paris   Tel. 01.45.78.12.92
                                Fax: 01.45.75.05.67

Gibert Jeune (Droit-Économie)
6, place Saint-Michel
75006 Paris   Tel. 01.43.25.91.19

Librairie du Commerce International
10, avenue d'Iéna
75016 Paris   Tel. 01.40.73.34.60

Librairie Dunod
Université Paris-Dauphine
Place du Maréchal-de-Lattre-de-Tassigny
75016 Paris   Tel. 01.44.05.40.13

Librairie Lavoisier
11, rue Lavoisier
75008 Paris   Tel. 01.42.65.39.95

Librairie des Sciences Politiques
30, rue Saint-Guillaume
75007 Paris   Tel. 01.45.48.36.02

P.U.F.
49, boulevard Saint-Michel
75005 Paris   Tel. 01.43.25.83.40

Librairie de l'Université
12a, rue Nazareth
13100 Aix-en-Provence   Tel. 04.42.26.18.08

Documentation Française
165, rue Garibaldi
69003 Lyon   Tel. 04.78.63.32.23

Librairie Decitre
29, place Bellecour
69002 Lyon   Tel. 04.72.40.54.54

Librairie Sauramps
Le Triangle
34967 Montpellier Cedex 2   Tel. 04.67.58.85.15
                                Fax: 04.67.58.27.36

A la Sorbonne Actual
23, rue de l'Hôtel-des-Postes
06000 Nice   Tel. 04.93.13.77.75
                                Fax: 04.93.80.75.69

GERMANY – ALLEMAGNE
OECD Bonn Centre
August-Bebel-Allee 6
D-53175 Bonn   Tel. (0228) 959.120
                                Fax: (0228) 959.12.17

GREECE – GRÈCE
Librairie Kauffmann
Stadiou 28
10564 Athens   Tel. (01) 32.55.321
                                Fax: (01) 32.30.320

HONG-KONG
Swindon Book Co. Ltd.
Astoria Bldg. 3F
34 Ashley Road, Tsimshatsui
Kowloon, Hong Kong   Tel. 2376.2062
                                Fax: 2376.0685

HUNGARY – HONGRIE
Euro Info Service
Margitsziget, Európa Ház
1138 Budapest   Tel. (1) 111.60.61
                                Fax: (1) 302.50.35
E-mail: euroinfo@mail.matav.hu
Internet: http://www.euroinfo.hu//index.html

ICELAND – ISLANDE
Mál og Menning
Laugavegi 18, Pósthólf 392
121 Reykjavik   Tel. (1) 552.4240
                                Fax: (1) 562.3523

INDIA – INDE
Oxford Book and Stationery Co.
Scindia House
New Delhi 110001   Tel. (11) 331.5896/5308
                                Fax: (11) 332.2639
E-mail: oxford.publ@axcess.net.in

17 Park Street
Calcutta 700016   Tel. 240832

INDONESIA – INDONÉSIE
Pdii-Lipi
P.O. Box 4298
Jakarta 12042   Tel. (21) 573.34.67
                                Fax: (21) 573.34.67

IRELAND – IRLANDE
Government Supplies Agency
Publications Section
4/5 Harcourt Road
Dublin 2   Tel. 661.31.11
                                Fax: 475.27.60

ISRAEL – ISRAËL
Praedicta
5 Shatner Street
P.O. Box 34030
Jerusalem 91430   Tel. (2) 652.84.90/1/2
                                Fax: (2) 652.84.93

R.O.Y. International
P.O. Box 13056
Tel Aviv 61130   Tel. (3) 546 1423
                                Fax: (3) 546 1442
E-mail: royil@netvision.net.il

Palestinian Authority/Middle East:
INDEX Information Services
P.O.B. 19502
Jerusalem   Tel. (2) 627.16.34
                                Fax: (2) 627.12.19

ITALY – ITALIE
Libreria Commissionaria Sansoni
Via Duca di Calabria, 1/1
50125 Firenze   Tel. (055) 64.54.15
                                Fax: (055) 64.12.57
E-mail: licosa@ftbcc.it

Via Bartolini 29
20155 Milano   Tel. (02) 36.50.83

Editrice e Libreria Herder
Piazza Montecitorio 120
00186 Roma   Tel. 679.46.28
                                Fax: 678.47.51

Libreria Hoepli
Via Hoepli 5
20121 Milano   Tel. (02) 86.54.46
                                Fax: (02) 805.28.86